D1250605

The Toyota
Management System

The Toyota Management System

Linking the Seven Key Functional Areas

Yasuhiro Monden

Publisher's Message by
Norman Bodek

Translated by
Bruce Talbot

Productivity Press
PORTLAND, OREGON

Productivity Press
P.O. Box 13390
Portland, OR 97213-0390
Telephone: (503) 235-0600
Telefax: (503) 235-0909

Book and cover design by Gary Ragaglia
Printed and bound by Edwards Brothers Incorporated
Printed in the United States of America on acid-free paper

Library of Congress Cataloging-in-Publication Data

Monden, Yasuhiro. 1940-
    The Toyota management system: linking the seven key functional
areas/Yasuhiro Monden; publisher's message by Norman Bodek; translated
by Bruce Talbot.
        p.   cm.
    Translated from the Japanese.
    Includes bibliographical references and index.
    ISBN 1-56327-014-5
    1. Automobile factories — Management.   2. Just-in-time systems.
3. Toyota Jidōsha Kabushiki Kaisha.
TL278.M66   1993
629.23'4 — dc20   92-27133
                                                                         CIP

        97 96 95 94   10 9 8 7 6 5 4 3 2

Contents

vii Tables and Figures

xi Publisher's Message

xv Preface

xix Introduction • A Unified System of Business Management: The Pursuit of Effectiveness

1 Chapter One • Financial Management System

29 Chapter Two • Target Costing and Kaizen Costing in the Japanese Automobile Industry

53 Chapter Three • Functional Management to Promote Companywide Coordination: Total Quality Control and Total Cost Management

71 Chapter Four • Flat Organizational and Personnel Management

87 Chapter Five • Sales Management System

101 Chapter Six • New Product Development System

131 Chapter Seven • Production Management System: Integration of SIS, CIM, and JIT

173   Chapter Eight • International Production Strategies
      of Japanese Automakers

205   Notes
209   Bibliography
215   About the Author
217   Index

Tables and Figures

Table 1-1.	Capital Procurement Trends, 1974-1988	4
Table 1-2.	Shares of Operating Profits and Finance-based Revenues	8
Table 1-3.	Detailed Data Concerning Toyota's Capital Applications	10-11
Table 1-4.	Total Capital Invested in Affiliated Companies	15
Table 1-5.	Capital Demand Statistics (BY74 to BY81)	20-21
Table 1-6.	Capital Demand Statistics (BY82 to BY88)	22-23
Figure 2-1.	The Target Costing System	34-35
Figure 2-2.	General New Product Plan	36
Figure 2-3.	Target Cost Broken into Cost Elements and Functions	38
Figure 2-4.	Target Cost Broken into Parts Elements	40
Figure 2-5.	Summary of the Target Costing Process	41
Figure 2-6.	Objectives Decomposition in Plants	48
Figure 2-7.	Example of Kaizen Cost Decomposition in a Machining Department	49

Figure 2-8.	Example of Kaizen Cost Decomposition in a Stamping Department	50
Table 3-1.	Quality Assurance Summary	56
Table 3-2.	Cost Management Summary	57
Table 3-3.	Summary of Various Functional Managements	59
Figure 3-1.	Framework of Toyota Management Organization (as of 1981)	63
Figure 3-2.	Six Elements of Business Policy at Toyota	66
Figure 3-3.	Toyota Planning and Control System	68
Figure 4-1.	Reforms to Accelerate Decision-making and Cultivate Employee Abilities	73
Figure 4-2.	Reorganization of Middle Management at Toyota	74
Table 5-1.	Sales Forces of Major Japanese Automakers	90
Table 5-2.	Toyota's Sales and Service Network	94-95
Figure 6-1A.	New Product Development Organization	105
Figure 6-1B.	Engineering Division Organization	106-107
Figure 6-2.	Development Schedule	109
Figure 6-3.	The Chief Engineer System Behind New Car Development at Toyota	110
Figure 6-4.	New Model Planning Process	111
Figure 6-5.	Prototype Process Flow	116
Figure 7-1.	TNS: Toyota's Strategic Information System	133
Figure 7-2.	Reception of Ten-day Orders from Dealers	136
Figure 7-3.	Steps from Dealer Orders to Line-off	137
Figure 7-4.	Parts Delivery Table	143
Figure 7-5.	Computer Control Functions in a Multilayered System	148

Figure 7-6.   Process-specific Line   150-151
               Computer Functions
Figure 7-7.   Magnetic Card   153
Figure 7-8.   Work Instruction Label   157
Figure 7-9.   Work Instruction with Specification   158
               Indicator Lamps
Figure 7-10.   Overall View of the New ALC   160-161
               System
Figure 7-11.   Outline of Toyota/   165
               JIT Production System
Figure 7-12.   Flow of Two Types of Kanban   167
Table 8-1.   Major Joint-venture Production Between   178
               Japanese and Western Automakers
Figure 8-1.   Differences Between Contracted   184
               Production, Technology Transfer,
               and OEM Production
Table 8-2.   Major Examples of Direct Production   185
               Expansion by Japanese Automakers in
               Europe and North America
Figure 8-2.   Current International Industrial Division   190

Publisher's Message

FOR OVER A DECADE, manufacturers have gazed wide-eyed while Toyota Motors has risen to astonishing heights. In the West, we study Toyota's production system with its just-in-time (JIT) and kanban methodologies and try to adapt it to our own workplaces. In truth, amony my reasons for founding Productivity Press was so that I could purchase English-language rights to the Japanese work of manufacturing giants such as Taiichi Ohno and Shigeo Shingo. These two early Toyota men were responsible for the development and ultimate success of this world-class manufacturer.

We all realize, of course, that Toyota's success is based on more than any single production technique. These days, in fact, it is difficult to think of Toyota in strictly manufacturing terms because it has gone so far beyond. Consider the breadth of its marketing and sales management, consider its new product development, financial management, international production strategy, and so on. Fortunately, Yasuhiro Monden does it for us in this fine book., *The Toyota Management System: Linking the Seven Key Functional Areas.*

Recognized worldwide for his knowledge of the Japanese automobile industry, Dr. Monden was instrumental in the early 1980s in bringing information about the JIT production system to the United States. He has written numerous books for Western readers, including the 1984 classic *Toyota Production System* and *Japanese Management Accounting: A World Class Approach to Profit Management*, which Productivity published in 1989. Currently professor of managerial accounting and production management at the University of Tsujuba, he has been a visiting professor at California State University in Los Angeles and at the State University of New York in Buffalo. He also serves on the editorial board of the American Accounting Association's Journal of Management Accounting Research. As these credentials show, Dr. Monden is a respected authority on both sides of the Pacific.

While much has been written about various aspects of Toyota's production system, this is the first book to examine the unified, all-encompassing management system to successfully evolve in the process. Eight chapters describe Toyota's financial management system; profit management; its companywide cross-functional management; its "flat" organizational system and personnel management; its dales management system; new product development; production management (and how it incorporated a strategic information system [SIS], computer-integrated manufacturing [CIM], and just-in-time methods); and, lastly, its international production strategy.

There is something here for people in all areas of a company — and for all kinds of companies. The wisdom that has evolved from Toyota's manufacturing environment is broader than one industry. It can serve many. Taiichi Ohno recognized this and talked about it in his book *Just-In-Time for Today and Tomorrow*. And now, we see just that. We find JIT ideas applied to restaurants (Kentucky Fried Chicken), convenience stores (7-Eleven), public utilities (Florida Power & Light), chemicals (Exxon), computers (Iomega), and communications (AT&T). The list goes on — but it would be better for you to read this book and consider how to apply it for yourself.

Nearly a decade ago I resolved to publish in English informative and sometimes provocative books by Japan's thinkers and doers in management and manufacturing. Japan's financial and industrial evolvement in the post-World War II and now post-Cold War era has made this of great importance to us globally and nationally. And I, among others, feel that we have much to learn about our Pacific neighbors.

As always, it takes many people to create a book and I wish to acknowledge them: Bruce Talbot, translator; Cheryl Rosen, acquisitions and project editor; Bill Berling, freelance copyeditor; Dorothy Lohmann, managing editor; Laura St. Clair, assistant editor; Jennifer Cross, indexer; David Lennon, production manager; Karla Tolbert, typesetter; and Gary Ragaglia, cover designer. I have known the author since 1980 when he addressed an American audience about the new Japanese manufacturing mentality. I have followed his progress since and speak for all us at Productivity in saying that we are honored to publish another of his fine books.

Norman Bodek
Publisher
Productivity Press

Preface

WHAT IS THE BEST way to develop, produce, and market goods and services? And how should a company raise the capital needed for investing in such an undertaking? How should costs be planned and managed to make sure the end result is "profitability?" What is an effective way to develop production and sales activities on a global scale? And how can the company develop an organization that enables employees to respond flexibly to their fast-changing environment?

Today, companies in many industries face management issues such as these. This book attempts to explain how companies can practice effective management as they undertake these basic management activities. I have decided to use the Toyota Motor Company as the sole source for the case studies contained in this book in order to describe more systematically one of the world's most effective management systems.

Many books have been written about Toyota's production management system, also known as the "Just-In-Time Production Method" (JIT). However, this is the first to present a comprehensive and systematic description of Toyota's entire management system, which includes not only production management but also research and development (R&D) management, sales management, financial management, cost planning, organizational management, and the planning of international production strategy.

The reader might question the need for a book describing Toyota's entire management system. I feel the necessity because Toyota's production management system is actually a subsystem that does not exist separately from the company's overall management system. The functions of these subsystems are mutually supportive functions, so that the production management subsystem exchanges support with the sales subsystem, new product development subsystem, financial management subsystem, personnel subsystem, and so on. This mutual support among subsystems is a key factor contributing to the excellent performance of Toyota's overall management system.

One point I have tried to emphasize in this book is the interdependence between *management functions* and *manufacturing functions*. To carry out its more socially significant function of making products, Toyota has integrated a wide range of management functions into its production system to make the production functions more effective in serving the needs of society. (This will also be addressed in the Introduction.)

This book's target readership includes — and goes beyond — the ranks of top managers who oversee large corporate organizations that encompass many skill categories. It is also intended for middle managers in each type of corporate division and skill category as a reference for improving their management activities. I am especially hopeful that this book will be read by production department managers because I feel they have much to gain by better understanding how peripheral departments relate to their own departments.

Finally, this book should be useful to students and employees aspiring toward management careers as a textbook on the latest advances in Japanese management methods and a systematic study of Japanese corporate management.

I will conclude by offering my heartfelt thanks to Mr. Kazuya Uchiyama of the Japan Management Association, who again has lent invaluable and extensive support in the publication of my work.

Introduction

A Unified System of Business Management: The Pursuit of Effectiveness

SINCE World War II, Japanese companies have pursued "effectiveness" as a chief management principle. Effectiveness means being able to respond to environmental changes and also to achieve the company's objectives in an efficient, waste-free manner. The strong competitiveness of Japanese companies in the global marketplace springs from the highly effective management systems these companies have developed. With its broad scope, the Toyota management system described in this book is a typical example.

Toyota Motor Corporation is involved in a wide range of activities and makes various kinds of contributions to society, the principal contribution being its role as a manufacturer of automobiles. In this book, we shall look into what functions Toyota carries out as an automaker, how it has woven various management skills into the fabric of its production system, and how Toyota's production functions effectively contribute to society.

To make "things," manufacturing company managers must first gather together and make effective use of human and financial resources; in other words, people and money. Accordingly, this study describes how managers prepare for production by procuring funds and how they manage those funds. We call this the financial management system.

Since the main objective in investing money is to make a profit, one of the manufacturer's functions is to minimize production costs to leave room for profits. We will examine the cost planning methods Toyota uses.

We will also see why companies need a personnel organization that both enables and encourages people to put energy and enthusiasm into their work.

After that, we will examine the strengths of Toyota's sales organization — its automobile sales network. Sales is a primary motivating force for manufacturing since there is no point in manufacturing anything unless the sales outlets are able to sell it. We will also look at Toyota's steps for new product development, its narrowly defined production steps, and its strategy for international production.

Following are brief summaries of each chapter's contents and how they tie in with manufacturing functions.

CHAPTER 1: FINANCIAL MANAGEMENT SYSTEM

The function of financial management is to achieve a balance between capital procurement and capital application. Manufacturing companies should not procure capital purely for the sake of security portfolio investment. At Toyota, each new car model requires a minimum investment of $365 million (¥ 50 billion) in new car development work and corresponding new equipment. How does Toyota come up with that kind of money? We will find out as we examine Toyota's capital procurement and application system for financing new products. In so doing, we will also study Toyota's approach toward managing security portfolio investment.

CHAPTER 2: TARGET COSTING AND KAIZEN COSTING IN THE JAPANESE AUTOMOBILE INDUSTRY

As a profit-oriented company, Toyota strives to realize a yearly net profit and seeks to return dividends to its shareholders. To ensure profitability, Toyota must supply funds for plant investment and other purposes. In order to achieve its long-term and annual profit targets, Toyota plans ways to keep costs down in a *target costing* system initiated at the new product development stage. Later, at the production stage, Toyota carries out a series of further cost-saving improvements in a *kaizen costing* system.

CHAPTER 3: FUNCTIONAL MANAGEMENT

While U.S. automakers have decentralized organizations composed of many profit center divisions, Toyota's organization is fully centralized. Therefore, the responsibility for establishing communication links between the various departments at Toyota and ensuring cooperation and coordination in implementing companywide quality control and cost management is given to an organizational unit called a *functional meeting*.

This is a top management decision unit that makes policy decisions and action plans for implementing in each department.

CHAPTER 4: FLAT ORGANIZATIONAL AND PERSONNEL MANAGEMENT

Toyota has introduced what it calls a "flat organization" in which the *just-in-time* approach has been applied to decision making among middle and lower managers throughout the company to prevent decision-making delays. We will examine the structure and operation of this flat organization.

CHAPTER 5: SALES MANAGEMENT SYSTEM

Sales is the function that enables the production function to operate. Smooth daily production of goods is only possible when certain large numbers of those goods can be sold. The number of goods sold is determined largely by the appeal of the goods themselves and by *sales strength*, which is a product of factors such as the number of sales outlets and the abilities of the sales and promotion people. This chapter will look at Toyota's sales strength and the special features of the Toyota sales network.

CHAPTER 6: NEW PRODUCT DEVELOPMENT SYSTEM

For automakers, the new product development system is the starting point in the process of creating new cars. This process begins with market surveys and new product planning and continues with exterior and interior design, body and main parts design, prototype fabrication and testing, line setup, and so on. For certain car models, Toyota designates a single person as the car's chief engineer; this person is responsible for the entire development process. This chapter examines how Toyota cars are designed and developed under this *chief engineer system*.

CHAPTER 7: PRODUCTION MANAGEMENT SYSTEM: SIS, CIM, AND JIT

How does the end user's order information flow between the car sales agent on the one hand and Toyota and its parts suppliers on the other? This chapter describes Toyota's *Strategic Information System (SIS)* that provides a network enabling such sales information to flow more efficiently. How does Toyota apply today's advanced data processing and electronic communications technologies to keep tabs on the equipment, people, and goods at its various assembly plants? The answer is Toyota's *Computer-integrated Manufacturing (CIM)* system that allows each factory to operate autonomously as it does under the famous *kanban* system. Finally, we examine the *just-in-time (JIT)* aspects of Toyota's Production Management System. This helps ensure that only products that can be sold reach the market, and that they reach the market only in the required amounts and at the required delivery time.

CHAPTER 8: INTERNATIONAL PRODUCTION STRATEGY

This chapter looks at the globalization strategies of Toyota and other Japanese automakers, including their international strategies for parts procurement.

On the whole, this book is intended to enlighten readers as to how Toyota links its activities with its primary social role as a manufacturer and how it achieves its primary goal of raising production effectiveness in its myriad forms, such as flexibility, quick responsiveness, productivity, and profitability.

CHAPTER ONE

Financial Management System

WHEN WE REFER to a company's financial management system we mean the decision-making process related to the procurement and application of capital. This chapter examines Toyota's financial management system.

Japan's business environment has undergone great changes, both during the oil crises of the 1970s and during the yen's steep climb against the dollar that began in the mid-1980s. These environmental changes have forced Japanese companies to become more dependent on capital from outside investors and more heavily burdened by interest obligations.

It sometimes happens that capital resources run dry, creating a life-or-death situation for the company. To avoid such predicaments, companies must build for themselves a financial structure that can withstand the kind of dramatic environmental changes that have occurred in recent years.

When the business environment is a favorable one, it is relatively easy for companies to procure both internal and external capital. The main purposes for such capital include funds for new plant investment, new product development, or for working capital. Any funds left over after serving these purposes usually are channeled toward safe and profitable investments in vehicles that lie outside the company's main fields of business.

During an economic recession or depression, companies must move to protect their main business activities. At such times they are also wise to put the funds accumulated through their effective management of capital assets during the economic boom years into short-term, high-yield investments that provide safe alternatives to main business investments. In fact, companies always need such external investments as a source of capital that can be readily channeled toward new business opportunities.

The point of the strategy just described is to stop looking outside the company for capital procurement and to instead use funds produced by the company itself. When the need for funds is large, however, these internal fund-raising methods may not be enough, and the company may decide to turn to fund-raising methods such as issuing convertible corporate bonds or warrant bonds (certificates with preemptive rights), methods which are likely to change the nature of the company's own capital assets. We refer to this type of financing as "equity financing," or capital procurement through new stock issues.

While acknowledging that the type of financial operations described previously varies somewhat from company to company and industry to industry, we can say with certainty that all companies work with the same basic rules, policies, and know-how in managing their financial operations.

This chapter analyzes the financial data of Toyota Motor Corporation, known today for its debt-free management and for its top ranking as a company that stays "in the black."

These data cover the years 1974 to 1988. We will look at how Toyota has procured and managed its capital assets to support its automobile production and sales organizations. Specifically, we will study the rules, policies, and know-how behind Toyota's financial management system and will identify the basic principles of its corporate financial operations.

SPECIAL FEATURES OF TOYOTA'S CAPITAL PROCUREMENT METHODS

What are the special features of the capital procurement methods used by Toyota? Table 1-1 shows Toyota's capital procurement trends over several years. As shown, Toyota clearly is oriented toward in-house capital procurement, for which it maintains vast amounts of retained profit and large depreciation expenses.

The retained profit reserves are what are left of the company's net (after tax) profits for each business term after the company allots dividends (including interim dividends) to shareholders and pays executive bonuses. From business year 1974 (BY74) to BY85, such retained income generally expanded. However, in BY78, BY79, and BY81, such funds shrank slightly from the previous year's level. The drop in BY78 was caused chiefly by the stricter controls on new-car exhaust emissions, the BY79 drop by the second oil crisis, and the BY81 drop by the Japanese auto industry's adoption of voluntary export restrictions on passenger cars sold in the United States and Canada. The slight reductions that occurred from BY86 to BY88 came under the impact of the yen's rapid appreciation against the U.S. dollar.

Depreciation expenses are the costs related to paying off the costs of depreciated items. As such, depreciation expenses are used to turn fixed assets into current assets or to recover invested capital. This makes depreciation expenses one of the

Table 1-1. Capital Procurement Trends (1974-1988)

| (External Capital) | | | | (Internal Capital) | | (unit: ¥1 million) |
Capital Increase	Increase in Corporate Bonds	Short-term Loans Outstanding	Year	Internal Retained Profit	Depreciation Expenses	Total: Cash Flow
28	0	0	49 (1974)	31,401	63,308	94,709
0	0	3,770	50 (1975)	61,323	127,468	188,791
22,834	0	569	51 (1976)	89,535	69,231	158,766
37,474	0	0	52 (1977)	101,802	61,231	163,033
44	0	0	53 (1978)	98,856	74,832	173,688
1	0	0	54 (1979)	83,328	90,054	173,382
32,554	0	0	55 (1980)	120,456	105,632	226,098
0	0	0	56 (1981)	107,767	121,005	228,772
99,051	0	0	57 (1982)	114,368	156,887	271,255
10,188	0	63,410	58 (1983)	164,682	173,456	338,138
0	0	0	59 (1984)	211,211	163,360	380,571
6,046	0	0	60 (1985)	260,865	174,373	435,238
6,347	0	0	61 (1986)	205,394	194,907	400,301
0	200,000	0	62 (1987)	150,421	220,259	370,680
2,480	117,760	0	63 (1988)	188,164	224,419	412,583

resources for in-house capital procurement. Although depreciation expenses declined slightly from previous-year levels in BY76, BY77, and BY84, on the whole they grew during the period of BY74 to BY88. The declines in BY76 and BY77 were caused by Toyota's curtailment of new plant investment in order to recover capital during the production slowdown that came in the wake of the first oil crisis.

We refer to the sum of a company's internal retained profits and depreciation expenses as the company's "internal capital." Analysts keep a close watch on the size of a company's internal capital as the company deals with changes in the economic environment.

At Toyota, there has been relatively little capital procurement from outside sources (that is, external capital). In fact, Toyota showed absolutely no external capital in its business results for BY81 and BY82, which underscores just how little the company relies on outside sources of capital.

Looking at more specific categories, we see that Toyota showed annual increases in short-term loans in BY75, BY76, and BY83. The BY83 jump, however, was caused by the merger of Toyota Motor Company with Toyota Motor Sales Company, an upturn that was reversed in the next year. Therefore, in real terms Toyota has operated under "debt-free management" (without a "loans" account title) since BY77.

Although Toyota's corporate bonds increased in BY87 and BY88, the corporate bonds issued in BY87 were U.S. dollar-based convertible bonds that were used primarily for meeting the funding needs of overseas projects such as the construction of assembly plants and other facilities in the United States. (As of 1992, one U.S. dollar equaled ¥ 130.) In BY88, ¥ 2.48 billion of these funds were converted to internal capital. Also in BY88, Toyota issued U.S. dollar-denominated warrant bonds which were also used for plant investments in

—————————————————

the United States. Because Toyota's results for BY88 were based on a business year that ended on June 30, 1988, neither the BY88 balance sheet nor the schedule of bonds payable showed Toyota's major bond issue of ¥ 30 billion in convertible bonds that took place on July 28, 1988, based on board decisions made on June 20 and July 11, 1988. Toyota issued these bonds to make use of the high yen and the voluntary car export curbs and as a manifestation of its U.S.-based projects that now covered activities ranging from capital procurement to automobile production and sales as operation of that capital.

Toyota shows a certain amount of fluctuation in its capital increases from year to year. Later in this chapter we will examine how capital operations (or meeting capital demand) relate to such increases. For the time being, please note which years have served as the main years for procuring new capital (such as BY77, during which Toyota raised ¥ 99 billion).

From what we have just observed, we can point to debt-free management and reliance on internal capital (especially retained profits) as the two primary special features of capital procurement at Toyota. These features did not change much even after 1986, when the yen's sharp rise against the U.S. dollar began making its full impact felt. This is because convertible bonds, unlike other liabilities, are converted easily into internal capital. Also the issuing of warrant bonds is a capital procurement method that facilitates the augmentation of internal capital.

Another special feature of financial management at Toyota is the way the company sells off short-term bonds and sets short bond maturity periods of less than a year as a well-timed method to procure short-term funds. To analyze this method, we must approach it from both the capital procurement and capital application perspectives, and we will do so later in the chapter.

SPECIAL FEATURES OF CAPITAL APPLICATIONS (RESPONSES TO CAPITAL NEEDS) AT TOYOTA

Previously, when we identified the two primary special features of capital procurement at Toyota, we noted the very strong emphasis Toyota puts on retained profits as an internal capital source. Table 1-2 shows the degrees to which operating profits from Toyota's main business and its finance-based revenues (non-operating profits minus non-operating expenses) based on financial activities have contributed to its net income before taxes.

In studying Table 1-2, please note the following definitions:

1. Share of operating profits = operating profits ÷ net income before taxes
2. Share of finance-based revenues = (non-operating profits − non-operating expenses) ÷ net income before taxes

While the main business (operating profit) continues over the years to dominate Toyota's net income before taxes, we still see a general rise in the share of finance-based (non-operating) revenues. This trend testifies to Toyota's relative stability in turning out successful results in its main business even when dealing with a changing economic environment. That is why we see much larger shares of finance-based revenues during years when total income before taxes are relatively low. In this manner, Toyota has responded to short-term depressions affecting its main business activities by strengthening the support provided by its financial activities. From this, we come to understand how Toyota has managed to be so strongly resistant to recessions in the automobile industry.

In other words, Toyota's strength in automobile manufacturing operations is backed up firmly by its skill in security portfolio investment.

Table 1-2. Shares of Operating Profits and Finance-based Revenues

(Unit: Percentage share × ¥1 million)

Business Year	Net Income before Taxes (Value)	Operating Profit		Finance-based Revenues	
		Value	Share (%)	Value	Share (%)
49 (1974)	45,608	22,903	50.2	15,857	34.8
50 (1975)	125,455	83,079	66.2	25,953	20.7
51 (1976)	192,659	148,561	77.1	37,509	19.5
52 (1977)	217,877	167,678	77.0	44,163	20.3
53 (1978)	206,786	153,082	74.0	45,721	22.1
54 (1979)	200,658	158,289	78.9	40,045	20.0
55 (1980)	288,668	233,232	80.8	58,348	20.2
56 (1981)	227,511	140,183	61.6	87,327	38.4
57 (1982)	298,489	230,513	77.2	75,670	25.4
58 (1983)	402,872	304,543	75.6	94,048	23.3
59 (1984)	516,767	406,482	78.7	115,285	22.3
60 (1985)	648,009	505,891	78.1	142,118	21.9
61 (1986)	488,385	329,387	67.4	158,998	32.6
62 (1987)	398,008	248,364	62.4	149,644	37.6
63 (1988)	521,706	369,087	70.7	152,619	29.3

Let us now look at the special features of Toyota's capital operations. Table 1-3 lists various detailed data concerning Toyota's capital operations. These data were compiled from annual securities reports for the period of BY82 to BY88, and all values are based on ledger balances, or book values, established immediately after June 30 — the end of each business year.

Table 1-3 lists Toyota's capital applications in the following three categories. We will examine their special features in greater detail.

1. applications in tangible fixed assets
2. applications in security portfolio investment outside of the main business
3. applications in support of affiliated *(keiretsu)* companies

APPLICATIONS IN TANGIBLE FIXED ASSETS

These are Toyota's investments in its main business. Most of these funds are used for plant investment. Between BY81 and BY87, the total funds in this category increased steadily until BY88, when tangible fixed assets dropped nearly ¥ 19 billion from their BY87 level. However, it probably will not be long before tangible fixed assets rise to reach the ¥ 1 trillion mark.

This type of main-business investment is needed to maintain a high level of production capacity and to help earn operating profits. As such, it is essential for the ongoing improvement of management and the development of the business. For automakers such as Toyota, main-business investment — especially plant investment for developing new car models — is the major investment theme for the company's financial managers.

APPLICATIONS IN SECURITY PORTFOLIO INVESTMENT OUTSIDE OF THE MAIN BUSINESS

Most of these funds are channeled into four types of investment vehicles:

Table 1-3. Detailed Data Concerning Toyota's Capital Applications

(Unit: ¥1 million)

Business Year (ending June 30)	56 (1981)	57 (1982)	58 (1983)	59 (1984)	60 (1985)	61 (1986)	62 (1987)	63 (1988)
(Tangible Fixed Assets)	582,352	615,954	735,682	722,293	768,293	929,393	982,119	962,966
(Working Assets)								
Cash Deposits	103,102	118,031	171,811	607,132	588,161	574,898	845,993	1,083,128
Securities	122,717	362,967	598,431	318,403	461,756	303,450	212,886	133,338
Investment Securities	196,207	184,628	213,352	260,216	281,478	295,348	334,035	365,840
Investment Stock in Affiliated Companies	148,370	162,191	163,481	186,251	203,416	221,588	258,710	344,685
Investment Bonds in Affiliated Companies	0	0	1,500	500	3,896	4,236	22,238	41,018
Contributions to Affiliated Companies	780	615	880	862	852	852	852	864
Long-term Loans Receivable from Affiliated Companies	6,897	5,978	20,184	23,912	23,246	25,045	31,689	13,738
Long-term Loans Receivable from Employees	42,167	47,708	62,778	67,715	65,761	60,938	51,816	12,083
Long-term Loans Receivable	8,482	6,905	26,819	23,785	19,446	18,360	18,150	21,960
Long-term Time Deposits	20,000	20,000	27,500	38,099	221,992	267,335	295,124	431,177

(Unit: ¥1 million)

(Breakdown of Cash Deposits)

Current, Ordinary, and Call Time	19,699	9,100	497,132	462,661	514,748	829,993	1,493
Time Deposits	83,332	156,211					1,046,905
Negotiable Time Deposits	15,000	6,500	110,000	125,000	60,150	16,000	0
Cash in Trust	0	0	0	0	0	0	34,730

(Breakdown of Securities)

Stocks	0	5	3	0	4	2	6
Public Bonds, Government Bonds, and Regional Bonds	362,967	598,426	318,399	461,756	303,446	212,883	133,331

(Breakdown of Investment Securities)

Stocks (for Affiliated Structure)	104,009	129,144	133,421	136,793	140,256	152,118	162,225
Public Bonds, Government Bonds, and Regional Bonds	75,375	76,530	120,229	136,295	145,130	173,810	193,177
Other	5,244	7,677	6,565	8,390	9,962	8,106	10,436

- cash and bank deposits
- securities (almost all are bonds rather than stocks)
- bonds as long-term investment securities
- long-term time deposits

CAPITAL APPLICATIONS IN CASH AND DEPOSITS The total amount of Toyota's cash and deposits took a major jump in BY84. In the wake of this big surge there were slight annual reductions in BY85 and BY86. However, cash deposits increased again in BY87, reaching nearly ¥ 85 billion; in BY88 they passed the ¥ 1 trillion mark. This put cash/deposits at a higher level than tangible assets for the BY63 term. Why did Toyota channel so much money toward cash deposits instead of main-business investments? We can see why by examining Table 1-3's cash/deposit breakdown. The four types of cash/deposits listed are: (1) checking, ordinary, and call deposits; (2) time deposits; (3) negotiable deposits; and (4) cash in trust. Note that in its annual securities reports for BY84 to BY87, Toyota lumped together the first two types.

If we compare time deposits for the years BY82 and BY88, we see that total time deposits were multiplied by a factor of 12.56 over this period. In BY88, they constituted almost 97 percent of the total cash deposits that exceeded ¥ 1 trillion. Undoubtedly, Toyota recognized the large-sum, variable-interest time deposits, first introduced in October 1985, as an attractive investment vehicle. Indeed, the further liberalization of Japan's finance and capital markets created many profitable new opportunities for time deposit investors. This explains why Toyota invested so much in time deposits over the years from BY84 to BY87.

Negotiable deposits offer the following five advantages: (1) they are freely negotiable, (2) they are variable-interest deposits with high investment yields, (3) they are sold in units of ¥ 50 million or above, (4) their time periods range from over two weeks to under two years, and (5) they are legally classified as deposits and exempt from Japan's securities transaction tax. Toyota made extensive use of this investment vehicle from the time it was introduced in May 1979. It soon owned such a large share of negotiable deposits that analysts began referring specifically to Toyota's share of the negotiable deposit market as the "Toyota rate." However, due to the later introduction of large-sum, variable-interest time deposits, Toyota's negotiable-deposit investments peaked in 1985 and then subsided rapidly before hitting zero in 1988. One reason for Toyota's abandonment of negotiable deposits was that they failed to earn interest after reaching maturity.

Toyota began to use the "cash in trust" investment method in 1988. This method, in which companies entrust cash to trust and banking companies who in turn invest it in stocks, bonds, and other vehicles, has gained popularity only recently in Japan. Since Toyota is known as a company that insists on safe high-yield investments, Toyota's financial experts no doubt have chosen only those trust and banking companies that specify exactly which kinds of vehicles they use for its entrusted funds. (Some trust and banking companies do not specify this.)

CAPITAL APPLICATIONS IN SECURITIES These are all short-term securities holdings, nearly all of which are bonds — either public bonds, government bonds, or regional bonds. Toyota has invested only ¥ 2 million to ¥ 6 million in stocks — relatively little indeed — and that has been largely in temporary acquisition of Toyota's own stock as required by fractional trading. These data reflect Toyota's securities policy of investing only in safe, high-yield bonds.

One method that has become popular among companies that are looking for short-term uses for ordinary surplus capital is the bonds with future resale value. Toyota has taken full advantage of what these investment vehicles have to offer. Bonds with future resale value are bought on the condition that they will be sold after a specified period of time. Their value can be determined freely, which makes them a variable-yield investment. The time periods for such bonds must not exceed one year, and actual transactions have been based on time periods ranging from a minimum seven days to a maximum of about six months, with a typical range of one to three months. The interest rate is set through negotiations with the relevant securities firms and banks prior to concluding the sale contract. Once the contract is signed, the terms are totally unaffected by stock market trends.

These conditions make temporary bonds a safe and reliable high-yield vehicle for very short-term investments that help the investor retain a high degree of liquidity. Naturally, temporary bonds have had to compete with other short-term investment vehicles. Since they are subject to the securities transaction tax, their yield has been slightly less than some other investment vehicles, such as negotiable deposits, that offer similar interest rates but are not subject to the securities transaction tax. These and other competing vehicles, such as large-sum, variable-interest time deposits, gradually lured Toyota away from temporary bonds. The result is that Toyota has invested only minimally in temporary bonds since 1985.

CAPITAL APPLICATIONS IN BONDS AS LONG-TERM INVESTMENT SECURITIES These are not temporary bonds but rather ordinary long-term bonds. Interest is paid to the bond holder each term until the redemption date when the principal is returned to the investor. This is what makes such bonds a convenient investment vehicle. Toyota's bonds in this category steadily increased between 1982 and 1988.

CAPITAL APPLICATIONS IN LONG-TERM TIME DEPOSITS This has been a fast-growing area of investment for Toyota since 1985, as Toyota has increasingly opted for large-sum, variable-interest time deposits. With time periods of one year or more, these time deposits have more restrictions than other investments that fall under the "cash deposits" category. However, banks sorely need time deposit investors as a key source of deposits. One would suppose that this supply-and-demand situation gives Toyota a strong hand when negotiating interest rates on such time deposits with banks. By 1988, Toyota's total investment in these time deposits exceeded ¥ 430 billion.

(unit: ¥1 million)

Year		Total Capital
57	(1982)	272,793
58	(1983)	315,189
59	(1984)	344,946
60	(1985)	368,203
61	(1986)	391,977
62	(1987)	465,607
63	(1988)	562,530

Table 1-4. Total Capital Invested in Affiliated Companies

SPECIAL FEATURES OF APPLICATIONS IN
SUPPORT OF AFFILIATED COMPANIES

The production and sale of automobiles entails a long series of processes. New model development occurs in unison with body and parts manufacturers because the major automakers depend so much on these supplier companies. They also depend heavily upon dealers when it comes to selling their products. Car sales generally involve finance companies as well. Most of these companies belong to Toyota's affiliate organization *(keiretsu)* and enjoy stable, long-term relationships with Toyota. Such affiliate relationships are vital to all Japanese automakers. As a result, Toyota's automobile business is operated by a group that includes Toyota and its affiliated companies.

Large amounts of capital operations must be devoted toward maintaining this organization. Refer to the five subcategories of capital applications that fall under this category in Table 1-3. These are:

1. stocks within long-term investment securities
2. investment stock in affiliated companies
3. investment bonds in affiliated companies
4. contributions to affiliated companies
5. long-term loans receivable from affiliated companies

Table 1-4 shows total funds that Toyota invested in support of its affiliated companies from 1982 to 1988. We can see a steady increase in these investments each year.

Looking at Table 1-3, we can see that Toyota's stock investments in affiliated companies (under the categories investment stock in affiliated companies and stock within investment securities) increased without exception year after year.

Almost all of Toyota's consolidated subsidiaries are dealer companies and 60 to 70 percent of its nonconsolidated subsidiaries are involved in the transportation industry. Toyota Motor Credit, a U.S.-based finance company, is a nonconsolidated subsidiary under the equity method. Japan-based Nippondenso, an auto parts manufacturing and sales company, is a nonsubsidiary affiliate in which Toyota Motor nevertheless owns a large equity share.

It is noteworthy that, during this period, the companies in which Toyota owned stock as investment securities included banks such as the Tokai Bank, Mitsui Bank, and Sanwa Bank, as well as various other companies across a wide range of industries.

As for the third subcategory, investment bonds in affiliated companies, Toyota first made these types of investments in BY83, then eased off from them the following year. It decided to increase them somewhat in BY85 and BY86 and then channeled more funds into them in BY87 and BY88. All such investments were in corporate bonds issued by affiliated companies.

The fourth subcategory, contributions to affiliated companies, includes both subsidiary and nonsubsidiary affiliates. The total here increased from ¥ 615 million to about ¥ 880 million.

As for the fifth subcategory, long-term loans receivable from affiliated companies, the total showed a sharp increase in BY83, stayed about even from BY85 to BY86, then rose again in BY87 before rapidly declining in BY88 as Toyota shifted funds toward other types of investments.

To summarize the special features of Toyota's capital operations: Toyota has been very active in capital operations involving tangible, fixed assets, which is only natural since these funds are devoted to Toyota's main business. However, Toyota has also been careful to establish strong resistance to recessions in the automotive industry by channeling surplus capital into safe, variable-interest investments outside of its main business.

With regard to capital operations outside of its main business, Toyota has responded expertly to changes in Japan's finance and capital markets and to the easing of restrictions and the appearance of new types of investment vehicles. Toyota has consistently concentrated such capital in investment vehicles that are conducive to highly effective capital operations.

Concerning its investments in affiliated companies, Toyota has recognized how essential it is that the entire Toyota group of companies be supported to help improve the flow of processes that includes delivery of materials and parts, production, distribution, sales, collection of fees, after-sales service, and so on, as well as the flow of related finance activities. This has required an increasing amount of investment from Toyota. When we examine the energetic way in which Toyota has invested in its affiliated companies, we can see that Toyota's management policy has been one of strengthening ties within the Toyota group and furthering the group's development.

THE RELATIONSHIP BETWEEN CAPITAL PROCUREMENT AND CAPITAL APPLICATIONS

The main theme of financial management in any company is the pursuit of corporate growth and profitability while maintaining financial stability in terms of balancing the company's capital procurement and capital operations. Tables 1-5 and 1-6 present capital demand data that describe how this balance between capital procurement and capital operations has been maintained over the years. (Table 1-5 presents Toyota business years 1974 (BY74) to BY81; Table 1-6 presents BY82 to BY88.)

The following is a year-by-year summary of the relationship between capital procurement and capital applications at Toyota.

- *BY74.* Still struggling to recover from the 1973 oil crisis, Toyota posted a low net profit and was unable to increase its tangible fixed assets due to a lack of retained profits. In addition, Toyota was forced to sell off some of its securities holdings to raise capital for meeting its obligations for corporate bonds, long-term debts, and other long-term accounts payable.
- *BY75.* Although it achieved a higher net profit this year, Toyota had to meet investment obligations that had been passed on from the previous year as well as its corporate bonds and long-term loans. The result was another year of capital shortages.
- *BY76.* Investment in tangible fixed assets dwindled to a mere 30 percent of the previous year's level as more surplus capital was channeled toward supporting affiliated companies. Toyota raised more capital for bond redemption and increased outlays to parts suppliers. A major improvement in total sales created expectations for greater sales volume. By way of preparation for this future volume growth, Toyota boosted its inventory assets investment 260 percent, and also achieved a shorter turnover period than in the previous business year. The net profit took a solid step upward. All in all, Toyota achieved a good balance in internal capital procurement and operations in BY76.
- *BY77.* Total sales increased 14.65 percent, a rate similar to the previous year's sales improvement. Much of the increased capital was channeled toward investment in tangible fixed assets, which grew 245 percent over the previous year. Meanwhile, investment in support of affiliated companies shrank to 60 percent of the previous year's level. Some funds also went toward bond

Table 1-5. Capital Supply and Demand Statistics (BY74 to BY81)

Business Year	49 (1974)	50 (1975)	51 (1976)	52 (1977)	53 (1978)	54 (1979)	55 (1980)	56 (1981)
Net Profit	39,147	73,841	99,559	116,777	116,286	102,058	143,568	132,727
Dividend Allotments (Subtracted)	7,616	12,294	9,844	14,755	17,180	18,480	22,802	24,640
Executive Bonuses (Subtracted)	130	224	180	220	250	250	300	320
Retained Profits	31,401	61,323	89,535	101,802	98,856	83,328	120,466	107,767
Depreciation Expenses (Added)	63,308	127,468	69,231	61,231	74,832	90,054	105,632	121,005
Cash Flow	94,709	188,791	158,766	163,033	173,688	173,382	226,098	228,772
Increase in Tangible Fixed Assets (Subtracted)	129,007	149,679	44,273	108,560	144,924	117,360	136,151	274,125
Capital Surpluses or Deficits	34,298	39,112	114,493	54,473	28,764	56,022	89,947	45,353
Reduction in Securities (Added)	54,186	208	0	0	9,880	0	0	150,064
Increase in Securities (Subtracted)	0	0	3,345	5,362	0	9,860	91,354	0
Balance Total	19,888	39,320	111,148	49,111	38,644	46,162	1,407	104,711
Increase in Investments and Other Assets (Subtracted)	4,448	7,454	43,903	26,032	8,878	37,233	87,709	56,874
Balance	15,440	31,866	67,245	23,079	29,766	8,929	89,116	47,837
Increase in Capital (Added)	28	0	22,834	37,474	44	1	32,554	0
Increase in Corporate Bonds (Added)	0	0	0	0	0	0	0	0
Increase in Long-term Accounts Payable (Added)	0	0	0	0	0	0	5,010	0
Other (Added)	0	0	0	0	0	0	0	0
Total	15,468	31,866	90,079	60,553	29,810	8,930	51,552	47,837
Reduction in Corporate Bonds (Subtracted)	2,256	3,636	4,300	4,152	4,152	0	0	0

Reduction in Long-term Loans (Subtracted)	601	272	0	0	0	0	0	0
Reduction in Long-term Accounts Payable (Subtracted)	284	0	79	0	4,941	401	0	4,973
Balance	12,327	27,958	85,700	56,401	20,717	8,529	51,552	42,864
Provision for Accrued Retirement Allowances (Added)	8,903	32,078	5,776	4,926	13,671	8,003	8,302	9,279
Appraised Loss due to Liquidation of Assets (Added)	0	1,375	1,558	1,940	0	3,183	4,625	4,389
Other (Added)	0	0	895	3,342	0	440	2,543	1,186
Total	21,230	61,411	93,929	66,609	34,388	20,155	36,082	57,718
Recovered Reserves (Subtracted)	2,988	33,448	9,421	8,457	9,283	10,324	7,088	3,715
Other (Subtracted)	0	22,130	894	690	59	0	3,463	2,924
Balance	18,242	5,833	83,614	57,462	25,046	9,831	46,633	51,079
Increase in Sales Credit (Subtracted)	1,056	80,815	54,390	40,003	60,427	49,383	47,064	41,317
Increase in Inventory Assets (Subtracted)	4,631	32,821	87,226	43,519	129	2,126	19,382	2,736
Increase in Other Fluid Assets (Subtracted)	2,148	2,442	74	1,821	958	483	192	144
Balance	10,407	110,245	58,076	27,881	36,210	42,161	113,271	12,354
Increase in Reserve for Bad Debts (Added)	0	4,305	1,247	1,030	858	0	906	1,129
Increase in Trade Payables (Added)	2,914	49,716	19,660	14,561	37,945	11,345	32,281	21,316
Increase in Short-term Loans (Added)	0	3,770	569	187	0	0	0	0
Increase in Other Short-term Liabilities (Added)	23,899	52,491	36,511	11,945	1,871	40,698	88,784	36,199
Increase in Cash Deposits	16,406	37	89	532	4,464	9,882	8,700	3,658

Table 1-6. Capital Supply and Demand Statistics (BY82 to BY88)

(Unit: ¥1 million)

Business Year	57 (1982)	58 (1983)	59 (1984)	60 (1985)	61 (1986)	62 (1987)	63 (1988)
Net Profit	141,589	201,372	251,567	308,309	255,185	200,208	238,006
Dividend Allotments (Subtracted)	26,901	36,270	39,897	46,972	49,319	49,319	49,334
Executive Bonuses (Subtracted)	320	420	459	472	472	468	508
Retained Profits	114,368	164,682	211,211	260,865	205,394	150,421	188,164
Depreciation Expenses (Added)	156,887	172,456	169,360	174,373	194,907	220,259	224,419
Cash Flow	271,255	338,138	380,571	435,238	400,301	370,680	412,583
Increase in Tangible Fixed Assets (Subtracted)	198,977	304,813	144,158	214,613	361,028	278,459	210,142
Capital Surpluses or Deficits	72,278	33,325	236,413	220,625	39,273	92,221	202,441
Reduction in Securities (Added)	0	0	280,031	0	158,306	90,564	79,548
Increase in Securities (Subtracted)	240,251	235,464	0	143,356	0	0	0
Balance Total	167,973	202,139	516,444	77,269	197,579	182,785	281,989
Increase in Investments and Other Assets (Subtracted)	5,065	87,616	84,890	219,159	73,637	121,940	218,829
Balance	173,038	289,755	431,554	141,890	123,942	60,845	63,160
Increase in Capital (Added)	99,051	10,188	0	6,046	6,347	0	2,480
Increase in Corporate Bonds (Added)	0	0	0	0	0	200,000	117,760
Increase in Long-term Accounts Payable (Added)	0	0	0	0	0	0	0
Other (Added)	0	268,999	0	0	0	0	0
Total	173,987	10,568	431,554	135,844	130,289	260,845	183,400
Reduction in Corporate Bonds (Subtracted)	0	0	0	0	0	0	2,480

Reduction in Long-term Loans (Subtracted)	0	0	0	0	0	0	0
Reduction in Long-term Accounts Payable (Subtracted)	0	228	0	0	0	0	0
Balance	73,987	10,796	431,554	135,844	130,289	260,845	180,920
Provision for Accrued Retirement Allowances (Added)	10,528	24,879	13,354	16,128	15,038	16,680	16,211
Appraised Loss Due to Liquidation of Assets (Added)	9,533	12,288	0	12,156	11,956	9,558	6,950
Other (Added)	1,770	0	18,049	3,701	0	2,661	53
Total	52,156	26,371	462,957	103,859	157,283	289,744	204,134
Recovered Reserves (Subtracted)	2,307	7,987	26,723	0	0	0	0
Other (Subtracted)	1,045	659	0	17,390	8,270	4,084	2,074
Balance	55,508	17,725	436,234	121,249	149,013	285,660	202,060
Increase in Sales Credit (Subtracted)	16,796	69,961	49,716	45,078	24,251	22,335	94,028
Increase in Inventory Assets (Subtracted)	7,554	90,096	15,964	3,293	30,264	18,356	8,444
Increase in Other Fluid Assets (Subtracted)	3,912	159,603	2,370	5,040	23,601	30,363	44,606
Balance	88,770	162,013	368,184	174,660	131,425	214,606	54,982
Increase in Reserve for Bad Debts (Added)	1,666	12,628	330	231	4,485	2,033	3,848
Increase in Trade Payables (Added)	8,836	69,613	27,758	21,643	15,683	4,830	39,863
Increase in Short-term Loans (Added)	0	63,410	63,410	0	0	0	0
Increase in Other Short-term Liabilities (Added)	88,197	70,142	102,459	134,277	155,886	63,352	138,442
Increase in Cash Deposits	14,929	53,780	435,321	18,971	13,263	271,095	237,135

redemption. BY77 was another well-balanced year for internal capital procurement and operations.

- *BY78.* Net profits were off slightly, but internal capital continued to expand. Investment in tangible fixed assets grew 133 percent over BY87. A little capital was siphoned off from securities investments and funneled into affiliated companies. Other capital went toward bond redemption and long-term accounts payable. Toyota achieved a major shortening of the turnover period for inventory assets. These and other results led to a cash deposit increase of ¥ 4,464 million.

- *BY79.* Both sales growth and net profits were down in the wake of the second oil crisis. Toyota responded by maintaining its main business at current levels. Accordingly, surplus capital was channeled toward investments in support of affiliated companies and buying more securities. As a result, cash deposits rose 220 percent over BY78.

- *BY80.* Toyota worked hard to improve its main business. It managed to recover from the second oil crisis and post an annual improvement in net profits. Sales jumped 18.12 percent over BY79. Some internal capital went toward increased investment in tangible fixed assets, but the bulk was channeled into investments outside the main business (particularly securities buying, which jumped roughly 927 percent) and toward affiliated companies. This created a capital shortage which Toyota met by raising more than ¥ 32.5 billion.

- *BY81.* Despite a slowing of sales growth, Toyota worked energetically to increase investment in tangible fixed assets. This led to an annual reduction in net profits. Because internal capital was not sufficient to cover this higher investment in tangible fixed assets,

Toyota sold off some of its extensive securities holdings to fill the gap. Toyota also disbursed funds into long-term accounts payable.

- *BY82.* This year, internal capital more than sufficed to cover investment in tangible fixed assets. However, Toyota also went on a securities buying spree and had to procure capital to cover these costs.
- *BY83.* The total sales figure soared as Toyota Motor merged with Toyota Motor Sales. However, this was not enough to meet all of Toyota's capital needs. The accounting results for BY83 are a complicated array of counterbalancing increases and reductions as a result of the big merger, and it is very difficult to analyze their overall significance. All short-term debts shown for this year were inherited from Toyota Motor Sales.
- *BY84.* Investment in tangible fixed assets were down from the previous year's level, which produced surplus internal capital that was funneled into paying off short-term loans and boosting investment in support of affiliated companies. Funds freed through securities liquidations were shifted toward negotiable deposits and time deposits. Net profits were up from the previous year.
- *BY85.* Net profits jumped 9.2 percent higher than the previous year's level. Internal capital left over after covering investments in tangible fixed assets were sent, along with some procured capital, into buying more securities and investing in support of affiliated companies.
- *BY86.* Tangible, fixed assets grew at their highest level in fifteen years. Internal capital, along with liquidated securities and procured capital, was channeled toward tangible, fixed assets and affiliated companies.

Cash deposits shrank due to a major disposition of reserves for short-term liabilities.

- *BY87.* Net profits plummeted under the impact of the yen's steep climb against the dollar. If we assume that almost all funds devoted to increased investment in fixed tangible assets went toward covering Toyota's U.S. dollar-denominated convertible bond issues, then the funds procured through securities sales were used for higher investments in support of affiliated companies and large-sum, variable-interest time deposits.

- *BY88.* Toyota began recovering from the high yen's impact. Net profits were up. All funds from the new corporate bond issues were used, along with some of Toyota's internal capital, to fill capital needs for increased tangible fixed assets investment, then the rest of the internal capital and the capital procured from securities liquidation went into outside investments such as large-sum, variable-interest time deposits, cash in trust, and support for affiliated companies.

CONCLUSION

Let us now summarize this chapter's presentation of the facts regarding Toyota's capital procurement and applications.

1. To a very large extent, Toyota has tended to procure capital through so-called internal capital which consists largely of retained profits and depreciation expenses. Even when Toyota turns to external sources to procure capital, such procurement is usually covered by owner's capital (stock) increases and convertible bonds. Consequently, we can recognize how Toyota has remained firmly committed to meeting its own capital needs in line with its policy of debt-free management.

2. To maintain and expand its capital from retained profits, Toyota has emphasized its positive support for plant investment, new car development funding, and investment in support of affiliated companies. Nevertheless, Toyota has also recognized the need for an external security net for its main business, which is very sensitive to economic downturns. Therefore, it also has pursued capital operations outside the main business that can be counted upon to remain profitable regardless of conditions affecting the automotive industry. Such operations have concentrated on investing in negotiable deposits; temporary bonds; large-sum, variable-interest time deposits; and other investment vehicles that offer safe, reliable, and high-yield returns. Toyota has been conspicuous for its strong aversion to stock-market investments. This conservative approach is seen as part of Toyota's staunch policy of putting its main business before all other considerations.

3. When increased investment toward tangible, fixed assets cannot be covered by Toyota's internal capital, Toyota has tended to liquidate some of its massive securities holdings.

4. Whenever Toyota has found itself with excess capital, it has tended to channel such capital toward further investments in support of affiliated companies or for acquiring more securities.

5. Whenever Toyota's main business has floundered amid depressed business conditions, Toyota has eased off on its tangible fixed assets investment and shifted more funds into outside investments and support for affiliated companies.

Finally, one point worth noting with regard to the relationship between Toyota's financial management system and its production management system is that the latter's success in drastically reducing inventory levels for materials, parts, in-process goods, and products has minimized the need to tie up funds in such inventory assets. This has contributed greatly to the company's financial management.

CHAPTER TWO

Target Costing and Kaizen Costing in the Japanese Automobile Industry*

ENVIRONMENTAL changes in the Japanese automobile industry are severe — for example, the high appreciation of the yen, the shortening of the product life cycle, the diversification of demand, and keen competition. Cost management methods must be useful for (1) the production of new products that meet customers' demands at lowest cost as well as for (2) the cost reduction of existing products by eliminating waste.

Therefore, companies today require a total cost management system that includes product development and design activities as well as production activities. This contrasts with traditional cost management, which focused on cost control in the production stage. The fact that most costs in the production stage are determined in the stage of new product development and design indicates the need for total cost management.

* This material, co-written by Professor Kazuki Hamada of Seinan Gakuin University, was first published in the Fall 1991 issue of *Journal of Management Accounting Research*. It is reprinted with permission.

This chapter describes the features of the total cost management system in Japanese automakers. Its two main pillars are *target costing* (establishing and attaining a target cost) and *kaizen costing*. They can be summarized as follows:

- *Target costing* (or *genkakikaku*) is the system to support the cost reduction process in the development and design phase of an entirely new model, a full model change, or a minor model change.
- *Kaizen costing* (or *genkakaizen*) is the system to support the cost reduction process in the manufacturing phase of the existing product model. The Japanese word *kaizen* differs slightly from the English word "improvement." Kaizen refers to the continuous accumulations of small improvement activities rather than innovative improvement. Therefore, kaizen costing includes cost reduction in the manufacturing stage of existing products. Innovative improvement based on new technological innovations usually is introduced in the development and design stage.[1]

Target costing and kaizen costing, when linked together, constitute the total cost management system of Japanese companies. "Total" cost management in this context implies cost management in all phases of product life. The concept of total cost management also comes from total involvement of all people in all departments companywide.

Since the concept of kaizen costing is rather new in the United States, we will clarify its concept, procedures, and relationships with target costing. The general idea seems to be that floor-level control activities are more useful in modern manufacturing plants as a result of the spread of the just-in-time (JIT) production system and total quality control (TQC), and that the accounting control system has become useless.

We would like to demonstrate, however, that the management accounting system functions well in both target costing and kaizen costing in Japanese automakers.

FEATURES OF TARGET COSTING

In broad terms, the step of corporate long- or middle-term profit planning is included in the process of target costing. A more narrow interpretation would have target costing consist of two processes roughly classified as: (1) the process of planning a specific product that satisfies customers' needs and of establishing the target cost from the target profit and targeted sales price of the new product, and (2) the process of realizing the target cost by using value engineering (VE) and a comparison of target costs with achieved costs.[2]

The basic idea of VE is that products and services have functions to perform and the amount of their value is measured by the ratio of these functions to their costs. By this process, the decision as to whether the product is to be produced is made. For this purpose, it is necessary that the functions of each product, part, and service are clarified and that all functions are quantified. For example, VE activities for direct materials can be implemented concerning the material quality or a grade change, the reduction of the number of bolts in a part, the change of a part shape, the common use of an alternative part, the change of painting method, and so on.

VE differs from control activities based on traditional standard cost accounting and it encourages the proposal of creative plans designed to reduce cost standards. This contrasts with standard cost accounting, which overemphasizes the determination and achievement of cost performance standards.

The VE techniques were first developed at General Electric by Lawrence D. Miles. In GE's case, however, they initially aimed at reducing the costs of purchased parts. Hence, their VE activities were not linked to corporate target profit and target costs as they are in Japan.

Target costing has the following general properties:

1. It is applied in the development and design stage and differs from the standard cost control system applied in the production stage.
2. Although it intends to reduce costs, it is not a management method for cost control in a traditional sense.
3. In the target costing process, many management science methods are used because managerial goals include the techniques of development and product design.
4. The cooperation of many departments is needed in its execution.
5. Target costing is more suitable in wide variety, small-lot production than in the mass production of a few products.

Other reasons why target costing has become important is that in Japan the ratio of variable costs to total manufacturing costs has increased remarkably in recent years (up to 90 percent in the auto industry); the ratio of direct material costs to total variable costs is about 85 percent. This means that the management of variable costs is increasingly important. Moreover, as the ratio of direct labor costs to total manufacturing costs is about 6 percent among automakers, managing direct material costs by target costing has become more important than managing direct labor costs.

Though the direct object of consideration in target costing is costs, target costing must be closely connected with corporate profit planning. Take for example, the case of a company that can develop products whose sales prices greatly exceed their high costs because of their high quality. If a company focuses only on costs, there may be a bias against high cost/high profit products. By linking target costing and profit planning, such a bias can be prevented. It also allows employees to understand that a company's ultimate goal is not cost reduction but higher profits.[3]

For our purposes we will divide the target costing process into the following five steps: corporate planning, developing the specific new product project, determining the basic plan for a specific new product, product design, and the production transfer plan.[4] Figure 2-1 outlines the target costing system.

THE TARGET COSTING SYSTEM

STEP 1: CORPORATE PLANNING

In Step 1, the long-and medium-term profit plans for the entire company are established and the overall target profit for each period is determined for each product. In the three-year profit plan, marginal income (sales price − variable costs), contribution margin (marginal income − traceable fixed costs), and operating profit (contribution margin − allocated fixed costs) as average figures for a series of developing models are computed. Based on this average figure, each of these three kinds of profits is planned for several representative types of each model. In computing operating profits, depreciation costs of facilities and dies, development costs, and prototype manufacturing costs are allocated to each model. Often the return-on-sales ratio is used to indicate the profit ratio for establishing target profit, because this ratio is computed easily for each product.

A corporate plan is drafted by the corporate planning department. As part of the process, new product development plans are drafted by the engineering planning department and a general new product plan is established. In this plan, the time frame of new product development, model

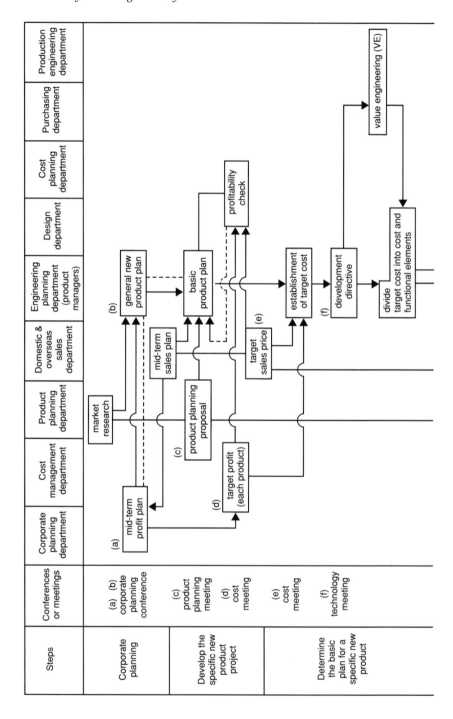

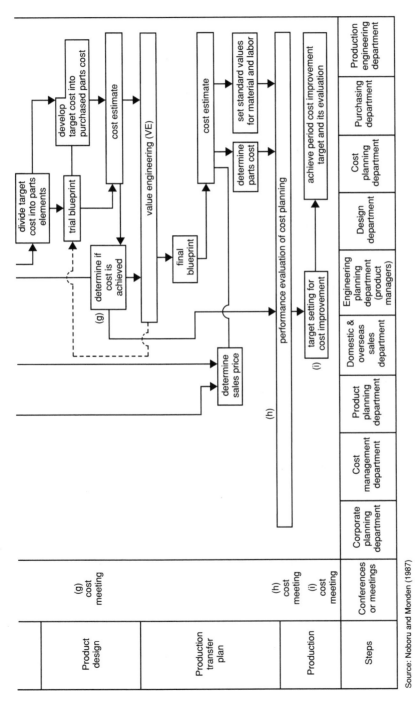

Source: Noboru and Monden (1987)

Figure 2-1. The Target Costing System

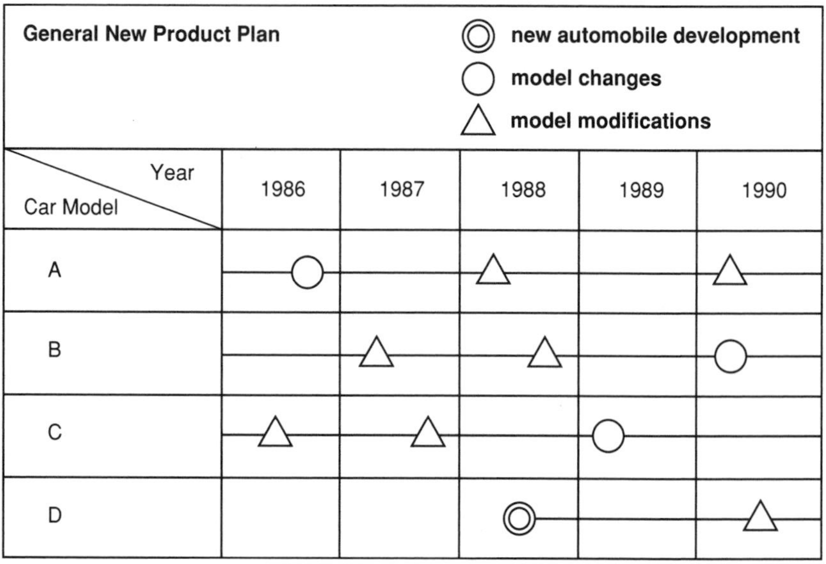

General New Product Plan		◎ new automobile development
		◯ model changes
		△ model modifications

Car Model \ Year	1986	1987	1988	1989	1990
A	◯		△		△
B		△	△		◯
C	△	△		◯	
D			◎		△

Source: Noboru and Monden (1983)

Figure 2-2. General New Product Plan

changes, and model modifications are established for all cars. This plan is illustrated by the form shown in Figure 2-2.

STEP 2: DEVELOPING THE SPECIFIC NEW PRODUCT PROJECT

In order to give shape to the general new product plan, the product planning department presents the engineering planning department with its wishes regarding the type of new product to be developed and the content of the model changes based on market research. This is discussed at the top management product planning meeting and the product planning proposal is prepared. The product manager later gives shape to this plan and establishes the basic product plan.

In this stage, the cost management department estimates the costs of the plan and investigates whether the plan can achieve the target profit. Some automakers use the payback period method as an aid in assessing profitability. The pay-back period normally covers no more than two model lives; that is, eight years. In the case of a specific facility used exclu-sively by a certain model, the payback period is usually no more than four years. For a minor model change the period is two years. One major company uses a simple accounting expenses measure (including interest costs) when deciding whether to add facilities. When the project does not appear profitable, the department requests modifications and elimi-nations. Only the profitable projects are adopted.

STEP 3: DETERMINING THE BASIC PLAN
FOR A SPECIFIC NEW PRODUCT

In Step 3, the major cost factors such as design and struc-ture are determined and target costs are established. The product manager requests each department to review material requirements and the manufacturing process, and estimate costs. According to the reports of the departments, the total "estimated cost" is computed.

At the same time, target price figures are gathered from the domestic auto division and the foreign auto division. From these prices and target profit, "allowable cost" is computed. The method of computation is as follows:

Target sales price − target profit = allowable cost

Allowable cost is the cost that top management strongly desires to attain. If this cost is adopted as the target of efforts, the requirement is very severe and not immediately attain-able. On the other hand, the estimated cost is not the appro-priate target of efforts. Thus, it is necessary to establish a "target cost" that is attainable and motivates employees to make efforts to ultimately achieve the "allowable cost." This is why studies and positive application of motivational fac-tors regarding employee behavior are needed.

Establishing the target cost needs to be reviewed on various dimensions regarding the size of the gap between allowable cost and estimated cost. Once the target cost is determined, and if that plan is approved, top management orders development based on it. Following that, each department implements VE activities regarding the design method in cooperation with each other in order to identify cost effective products that will fulfill customers' demands.

In addition, the engineering planning department decomposes the target cost into each cost element and functional element with the help of the cost management department.[5] Cost elements are material costs, purchased parts costs, direct labor costs, depreciation costs, and so on. Functional elements

Cost Elements / Functions	Material Costs	Purchased Parts Costs	Direct Labor Costs	. . . . .	Total
Engine	$	$	$		$
Transmission System					
Chassis					
(Etc.)					
Total					

The amount should be presented either in the form of the total cost for a single car (in the case of a new model or model change) or as a deviation from the existing model (in the case of model modifications).

Source: Noboru and Monden (1983)

Figure 2-3. Target Cost Broken into Cost Elements and Functions

are engine, transmission system, chassis, and so on. Important points are clarified by these detailed classifications. The form of the classification is shown in Figure 2-3.

The design department also decomposes the target cost into each part. This classification is made to be followed up by target achievement activities in the production design stage including the purchasing department. For this reason, the classification is detailed. The form of the classification is shown in Figure 2-4.

STEP 4: PRODUCT DESIGN

The design department drafts a trial blueprint according to the target cost set for every part. For this draft, information from each department is needed. The design department also actually makes a trial car according to the blueprint and the cost management department estimates its costs.

If there is a gap between the target cost and the estimated cost, the departments execute the VE analysis in cooperation with each other and the trial blueprint is adjusted accordingly. After repeating this process several times, the final blueprint is established.

STEP 5: THE PRODUCTION TRANSFER PLAN

Here, the preparatory condition of production equipment is checked and the cost management department estimates costs according to the final blueprint. The production engineering department establishes standard values of material consumption, labor hours, and so on. Those values are presented to the factory.

Those standard values are used as a data base for computing costs for the purpose of financial accounting and for material requirements planning (MRP). Therefore, they usually are fixed for one year. One major firm calls this value the "basic

Function			Assembly Number					Name		Direct Labor Cost		
	Part Number	Part Name	Quantity	Process	Car Model			Material Cost	Purchased Part Cost	Department	Worker Hours (Minimum)	Amount
Major Units					A	B	C					
									$	$		$

Source: Noboru and Monden (1983)

Figure 2-4. Target Cost Broken into Parts Elements

cost." The purchasing department also starts negotiating the prices of purchased parts at this time.

Soon after the target cost is set, production begins. The performance evaluation of target costing then is implemented after new cars have been produced for three months, as abnormal values usually arise during the first three months.

The performance evaluation of target costing is implemented to examine the degree to which the target cost is achieved. If the target cost is not achieved, investigations are made to clarify where the responsibility lies and where the gap arises. These investigations also evaluate the effectiveness of the target costing activities.

These are features of the target costing process used by Japanese automakers. In this process, summarized in Figure 2-5, management accounting plays an important role.

As target costing deals with the development and design of new products, many technical methods of engineering are needed. However, the management accounting system is important in effectively determining target profits, target costs and estimated costs.

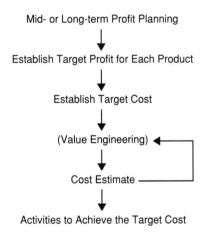

Mid- or Long-term Profit Planning

↓

Establish Target Profit for Each Product

↓

Establish Target Cost

↓

(Value Engineering) ◄———┐

↓ |

Cost Estimate ————————┘

↓

Activities to Achieve the Target Cost

Figure 2-5. Summary of the Target Costing Process

FEATURES OF KAIZEN COSTING

When Japanese accountants hear the words "kaizen costing" they expect a relation to the cost control system based on standard cost accounting. However, kaizen costing in the Japanese automobile industry has not been implemented according to standard costing. This means that the companies do not implement the traditional cost variance analysis based on the gap between the standard cost and the actual cost for each period. Kaizen costing is implemented outside the standard cost system as part of the overall budget control system. In essence, the actual cost per car for the latest period is the kaizen cost budget, which must be reduced in each successive period in order to meet the target profit.

The reason why Japanese automakers implement kaizen costing outside the standard cost accounting system is not because cost reduction in the production stage is taken less seriously, but because it is considered to be very important. Standard costing is limited by its financial accounting purpose in Japanese automobile companies and therefore it has many unsuitable features for cost reduction in the manufacturing phase.

Further, the concept of kaizen costing covers broader meanings than the traditional cost control concept that refers to meeting cost performance standards and to investigating and responding when those standards are not met. Kaizen costing activities include cost reduction activities that require changes in the way the company manufactures existing products. The inadequacy of standard costs for kaizen costing purposes is obvious from the viewpoint of "kaizen" concepts. Also the standard costs are changed only once a year.

Roughly classified, kaizen costing activities are of two kinds. One consists of activities implemented to kaizen actual performance when the difference between actual cost and target cost is large after new products have been in production for three months. The other kind consists of activities implemented continually every period to reduce any difference between target and estimated profit and, thus, to achieve "allowable cost."

In the former case, a special project team called a "cost kaizen committee" is organized and the team implements VE activities. The following distinction between VE and Value Analysis (VA) can be made. VE is the cost reduction activity that involves basic functional changes in the new product development stage. VA is the cost reduction activity that involves design changes of existing products.[6] However, the distinction is not made in this case and the term *VE* is used. Establishing a cost kaizen committee implies that the car model's kaizen is a top priority.

The following is a real life example of activities of the cost kaizen committee. Just after the oil shock in 1973, the profitability of one automobile model showed a marked decrease because of cost increases due to oil. At that time, the plant manager made the following proposals to the top management meeting concerning cost reduction:

1. Establish a cost kaizen committee chaired by the plant manager.
2. Promote a companywide cost reduction program for the specific model.
3. As substructures to this committee, organize the following three subcommittees:
   • production and assembly
   • design and engineering
   • purchasing
4. Establish a cost reduction goal of $75 per automobile.

5. Expect that the previous goal would be achieved within six months.

Through a concerted effect by all departments based on the decisions of the cost kaizen committee, the actual result of the plan was 128 percent attainment of the goal at the end of six months.

The second category of kaizen costing means reaching cost reduction targets established for every department as a result of the short-term profit plan. Different methods are adopted because of the difference between variable and fixed costs. For example, the variable costs such as direct materials, coating, energy, and direct labor costs are managed by setting the amount of kaizen cost per unit of each product type. Fixed costs are subjected to Management by Objectives (MBO) based on the overall amount of kaizen cost instead of the amount of kaizen cost per car.

The purchasing department supervises the purchase prices of parts from outside suppliers. In the factory the most important subject is the use of VE activities to reduce consumption. Usually, the purchasing department is not allocated an amount of kaizen cost target for its own department expenses, but attempts to reduce costs of parts by promoting VE proposals of vendors as well as by negotiating prices with vendors.

As for direct labor costs, monetary control as well as physical control in terms of labor hours is implemented by using the cost decrease amount as the kaizen cost target. A similar approach is applied to material costs improvement.

It is much easier for factory workers to understand the kaizen targets when the amount of cost reduction targets for both fixed and variable costs are presented individually rather than presenting the total cost target. Now we will consider the method of computation for the second category of kaizen costing.

COMPUTING THE TARGET AMOUNT
OF KAIZEN COST

Japanese automakers determine the amount of profit improvement (kaizen profit) based on the difference between target profit (planned by a top-down approach) and estimated profit (computed as a bottom-up estimate). They usually intend to achieve half of that amount by sales increases and half by cost reduction.[7] Of course, when the industry experiences an oil crisis or the high appreciation of currency, greater weight will be imposed on cost reduction.

They reason that the increase in sales increases profit, based partly on the notion of profit contribution. They also reason, based on the idea of ROI, that the sales increases raise the total asset turnover ratio. However, a sales increase can be generated by raising the sales price or increasing sales volume. The former does not cause an increase in variable costs, whereas the latter does.

For generating cost savings, reductions of both variable costs and fixed costs are considered. As most of manufacturing fixed costs are needed for maintaining continuous growth, Japanese automakers generally think that the amount of kaizen cost in the plants should be achieved mainly by reducing variable costs, especially direct material costs and labor costs.

However, in the nonmanufacturing departments, the amount of kaizen cost (or kaizen expense) reduction is set for fixed costs. Departments affected include the head office, research and development, and sales. The design department is usually not assigned an amount of kaizen cost. Also the purchasing department is not assigned one except in special cases such as an oil crisis or a yen appreciation.

The total amount of kaizen costs in all plants, which is (C) in the following formulas, is determined in the cost kaizen meeting as follows:

$$\text{Amount of actual cost per car in last period (A)} = \frac{\text{amount of actual cost in last period} +}{\text{actual production in last period}}$$

$$\text{Estimated amount of actual cost for all plants in this period (B)} = \frac{\text{amount of actual cost per car in last period (A)} \times}{\text{estimated production in this period}}$$

$$\text{Target of kaizen cost in this period = for all plants (C)} = \frac{\text{estimated amount of actual cost for all plants in this period (B)} \times}{\text{target ratio of cost decrease amount to the estimated cost}}$$

The target ratio of cost decrease amount to the estimated cost is determined in consideration of attaining the target profit of the year. That ratio is usually around 10 percent. For a new product, the target cost determined in the target costing process is expected to be attained within three months from the time production is started on the new product. After that, the figure can also be reduced further by applying the same technique of kaizen costing.

The target amount of kaizen cost assigned to each factory is as follows:

$$\text{Assignment ratio (D)} = \frac{\text{costs directly controlled by each plant}}{\text{total amount of costs directly by plants}}$$

$$\text{Total amount of kaizen cost for each plant} = \frac{\text{target of kaizen cost in this period for all plants (C)} \times}{\text{assignment ratio (D)}}$$

Cost directly controlled by a plant include direct material costs, direct labor costs, variable overhead costs, and so on. Excluded are the fixed costs such as depreciation costs. The amount of kaizen cost for each plant is decomposed and assigned to each division and that amount is again assigned to smaller units of the organization. Some details about the method of assignment are considered next.

The kaizen cost target is achieved by daily kaizen activities. The JIT production system also intends to reduce various wastes in the plant by these daily activities. Therefore, kaizen costing and the JIT production system are closely related with each other.

KAIZEN COSTING THROUGH "MANAGEMENT BY OBJECTIVES"

Each manufacturing plant has objectives about efficiency, quality, cost, and so on. The concrete targets of physical objectives are determined and evaluated in the production meeting, while kaizen cost targets are determined and evaluated in the kaizen cost meeting.

The cost meetings are held at several organizational levels; for example, at the plant, division, department, section, and process levels. In the meetings for each level, the amount of kaizen cost — that is, the amount of the reduction target — is assigned through Management by Objectives (MBO) at that organizational level.[8] That assignment is called "objectives decomposition" and is implemented according to concrete purposes and policies determined in advance.

However, it is essential that the objectives decomposition not be implemented uniformly, but based on the specifics of each case. Moreover, the determination of each objective, the evaluation, countermeasures, and so on, must be implemented flexibly depending on the specific situation. The outline of objectives decomposition in the plant is shown in Figure 2-6.

Figure 2-7 shows an example of objectives decomposition for attaining the kaizen cost target in a machining

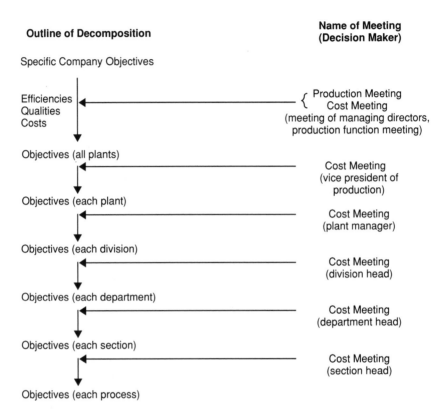

Figure 2-6. Objectives Decomposition in Plants

department.[9] Figure 2-8 is another example in a stamping department.

In Figure 2-7, managers at each organizational level determine policies and means to attain the kaizen cost target in their department. Their policies and means are mostly nonmonetary measures, but the purpose is to realize the kaizen cost target.[10] Managers at each level try to reduce actual labor hours, whereas the accounting department computes the actual labor costs and overhead based on these actual hours. Then actual labor hours and actual labor costs at each organizational level are publicized each month and the result is

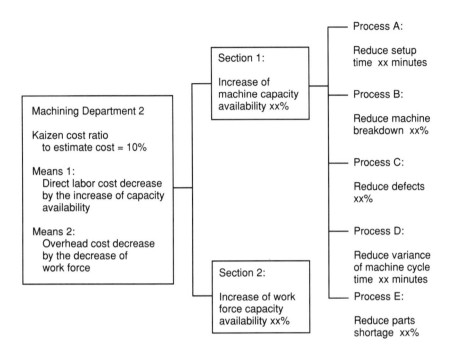

Figure 2-7. Example of Kaizen Cost Decomposition in a Machining Department

reflected via incentive pay in the salaries of the employees. This is quite a motivation. Thus, both production management and accounting control are functioning at the same time in the company.

In the floor-level control activities, the JIT production system has contributed remarkably to the reduction of costs. It is a system that reduces costs by thoroughly excluding waste in plants. Reducing inventories makes managers clarify many problems in plants. If inventories are reduced, the possibility of line-stops arising becomes higher in problematic places. This forces cost reductions by investigating causes of line-stops via defective units, machine breakdowns, and so on.

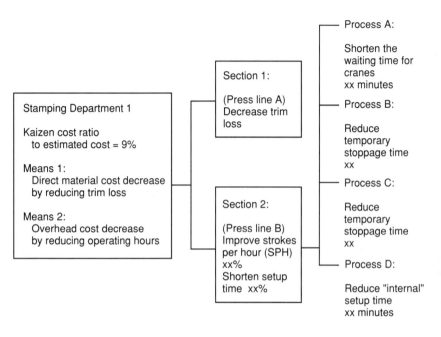

Figure 2-8. Example of Kaizen Cost Decomposition in a Stamping Department

As indicated, through the kaizen costing process, accounting control is used for assigning kaizen cost targets to plants, divisions, departments, and so on. The production and quality control by nonmonetary measures is used for floor-level control activities. On the manufacturing floor, everyone is involved daily in kaizen activities such as QC circles and suggestion systems. Thus, in Japanese automobile companies, accounting controls as well as floor-level controls are integral parts of the kaizen costing process.

MOTIVATIONAL CONSIDERATIONS IN TOTAL COST MANAGEMENT

It is necessary to be aware that target costing may force unreasonable demands on employees. As noted previously, motivational considerations must be considered for the attainability of target costs.

In kaizen costing activities, it is imperative to determine adequately the amount of the kaizen cost target and to assign adequately that amount for each division, department, and so on. It is important that the assignments of the amount are not overly affected by the organizational power structure. Rather, the "self-control" principle (autonomous management by each employee group) should prevail and each target should be determined through consultation between manager and subordinates.

For effective implementation of target costing and kaizen costing, each employee must tackle cost reduction positively. The company needs to devise methods that motivate employees to achieve their targets. Moreover, as VE activities require access to many kinds of information in various departments, methods that promote group activities and cooperation need to be adopted.

As the top row of Figure 2-1 shows, people in all departments are involved in target costing. This includes the purchasing department and suppliers — although the product manager of each model in the engineering planning department assumes major responsibility throughout development and design stages. The product manager plays the role of project leader in a matrix management system. As we also see in Figure 2-6, people in every level of the plant are involved in attaining the kaizen cost target. Thus, *people involvement* is very important in Japanese companies for executing target costing as well as kaizen costing.

SUMMARY

We have considered a total cost management system that includes product development and design activities as well as manufacturing activities. Specifically, we have examined the features of target costing and kaizen costing, which are the primary pillars supporting the total cost management system in all phases of the product life cycle of an automobile.

Although the importance of target costing is currently increasing, kaizen costing should not be slighted. Kaizen costing differs entirely from standard costing in that its goal is the continuous reduction of costs in the manufacturing stage. This is in contrast to standard costing, which aims to achieve and maintain standard costs. Target costing and kaizen costing should be inseparable from one another. If either is ignored, total cost management throughout the whole life of a product cannot be implemented adequately.

Functional Management to Promote Companywide Coordination: Total Quality Control and Total Cost Management *

TOYOTA'S organization is quite centralized, whereas U.S. motor companies have many decentralized units, called divisions, for each car line which is treated as a profit center. Thus, the responsibility for establishing communication links and coordination between the various departments at Toyota is given to an organizational entity known as a *functional meeting*. Functional meetings do not serve as project teams or task forces. Rather, they are formally constituted, decision-making units whose power cuts across department lines and controls broad corporate functions. Consisting typically of department directors from all parts of the company, each functional meeting will consider such corporate-wide problems as cost management, production management, and quality assurance (QA). The meeting then communicates their policy decisions and plans for

---

* This chapter is a revised version of one appearing in the author's book *Toyota Production System*, 2nd edition, published by the Industrial Engineering and Management Press in Norcross, Georgia. It is reprinted with permission.

implementation to each department for action. Such management through functional meetings is called functional management (*kinohbetsu kanri* at Toyota).

In this chapter, we will examine the structural relationships between the functional meetings and the more formally developed organizations at Toyota, how business policy is made and administered through functional management, and some of the advantages to be gained from the functional management concept. Although the Toyota production system in a narrow sense does not include the product planning and design steps, the author includes functional management in the broad overview of the system. The reader should realize that the most important aspects for increasing productivity or decreasing costs and improving quality are the quality control (QC) and cost reduction activities in the product development and design steps.

Historically, functional management is the outgrowth of a long process of trial and error. The QC Promoting Office at Toyota took the first steps toward companywide QC in 1961 by defining various important functions to be performed by the company. Each department, in turn, collaborated to determine and arrange the contents of the functions. By the addition, integration, and abolition of these inputs, the defined functions were classified and selected into the two most necessary rules for the entire company: quality assurance and cost management. Rules were then established to define what kinds of activities each department must undertake to properly perform these two functions.

QUALITY ASSURANCE

Quality assurance, as defined at Toyota, is to assure that the quality of the product promotes satisfaction, reliability, and economy for the consumer. This rule outlines the activities of each department for quality assurance at all phases from product planning to sales and service. Further, the rule specifies when and what should be assured by whom at where.

The rule defines "when" as eight applicable steps in a series of business activities from planning through sales: product planning, product design, manufacturing preparation, purchasing, manufacturing for sales, inspection, sales and service, and quality audit. The term "by whom at where" means the specific department manager and name of the department. "What" consists of items to be assured and the operations for assurance. Table 3-1 defines the quality assurance rule as it pertains to the steps in the business activities defined here and the primary operations of each department.

COST MANAGEMENT

Toyota utilizes cost management to develop and perform various activities to attain a specific profit goal, evaluate results, and take appropriate action as necessary. In other words, cost management is not simply confined to cost reduction. It also covers companywide activities to acquire profit. This rule specifically outlines the activities of each department level to maintain cost management. The framework of this cost management evolves from the following four categories: cost planning, capital investment planning, cost maintenance, and cost improvement.

Cost planning has been regarded as especially important because most of the cost is determined during development stages of the product. A cost planning manual assigns primary responsibilities and tasks at each phase of product development. Establishing a target cost to be followed during all development stages promotes activities to reduce costs, while maintaining minimum quality standards.

Table 3-1. Quality Assurance Summary

Functional Steps	Person in Charge	Primary Operations for QA	Contri-bution

Product Planning	• Sales department manager
	• Product planning department head
		1. Forecasts of demands and market share
		2. Obtain the quality to satisfy marketing needs
		  • Set and assign proper quality target and cost target
		  • Prevent recurrence of important quality problems
			△
			◎

Product Design	• Design department manager
	• Body-design department manager
	• Engineering department managers
	• Product design department manager
		1. Design prototype vehicles
		  • Meet quality target
		  • Test and examine car for:
		    performance
		    safety
		    low pollution
		    economy
		    reliability
		2. Initial design to confirm necessary conditions for QA
			◎
			○
			
			○

Manufacturing Preparation	• Engineering department managers • QA department manager • Inspection department managers • Manufacturing department manager	1. Prepare overall lines to satisfy design quality 2. Prepare proper inspection methods 3. Evaluate initial prototypes 4. Develop and evaluate a plan of initial and daily process control 5. Prepare line capacities	◎ ○ ○ △ ◎
Purchasing	• Purchasing department managers • QA department manager • Inspection department managers	1. Confirm qualitative and quantitative capabilities of each supplier 2. Inspect initial parts supplied for product quality 3. Support the strengthening of QA system of each supplier	△ △ △
Manufacturing	• Manufacturing department managers • Production control department manager	1. Match product quality to established standards 2. Establish properly controlled lines 3. Maintain necessary line capacities and machine capacities	○ ○ ○
Inspection	• Inspection department manager • QA department manager	1. Inspect initial product for quality 2. Decide whether to deliver product for sale	○ ◎
Sales and Service	• Sales department manager • Export department manager • QA department manager	1. Prevent quality decline in packaging, storage, and delivery 2. Education and public relations 3. Inspect new cars 4. Get feedback and analyze quality information	○ △ △ ◎

Table 3-2. Cost Management Summary

Functional Steps	Related Departments	Cost Management Operations	Contribution
Product Planning	• Corporate planning • Product planning office • Production engineering departments • Accounting departments	1. Set target cost based on new product planning and profit planning, then assign this target cost to various cost factors 2. Set target investment figures 3. Allocate target cost to various design departments of individual parts (cost planning or target costing) 4. Allocate target investment amounts to various investment planning departments (capital budgeting)	◎ ◎ ○ ○
Product Design	• Product planning office • Engineering departments	1. Estimate cost based on prototype drawing 2. Evaluate possibility of attaining target costs 3. Take necessary steps to minimize deviations between target costs and estimated costs through Value Engineering (VE)	◎ ◎ ○
Manufacturing Preparation	• Product planning office • Engineering departments • Manufacturing engineering departments • Production control department	1. Establish cost estimate by considering line preparation and investment plans 2. Evaluate possibility of attaining target costs 3. Take actions to minimize deviations 4. Evaluate facilities investment plans 5. Evaluate production plans, conditions, and decisions to make or buy parts	◎ ◎ ◎ ◎ ○
Purchasing	• Purchasing departments	1. Evaluate procurement plans and purchasing conditions 2. Establish control of supplier prices (compare target reduction and actual reduction amounts, analyze variances, and take appropriate action) 3. Investigate improvement of supplier costs [(apply Value Analysis (VA), establish support to promote supplier cost improvement activities)]	○ ○ ◎
Manufacturing Inspection	• Related departments • Accounting department	1. Instigate cost maintenance and improvements (kaizen costing) through the following: • budgeting fixed costs (manufacturing and managerial departments) • cost improvements in primary projects (classified for each type of vehicle and cost factor) • increased cost consciousness of employees through suggestion systems, case presentations, incentive programs, etc.	○ ○ ◎
Sales and Service	• Related departments • Accounting department	1. Measure actual costs of new products through overall evaluation 2. Participate in analyses and discussions at operations check, cost management functional meetings, cost meetings, and various committee meetings	○ ○

Cost maintenance and improvement are cost management processes at the manufacturing level. These are promoted by a companywide budgeting system and the improvement activities described in Chapter 2. To maintain these functions, each department has its own departmental budgeting manual and cost improvement manual.

The contents of cost management activities are specified in detail in the cost management operations assignment manual. Table 3-2 summarizes the cost management rule with respect to related departments and cost management operations.

RELATIONS AMONG DEPARTMENTS, STEPS IN BUSINESS ACTIVITIES AND FUNCTIONS

In order to effectively promote functional management, it must be clearly understood how each step to be performed by each department contributes to its function. Because equal emphasis cannot be placed on all operations, each step must be graded for relative contribution. Thus, the right-hand column in Tables 3-1 and 3-2 describes the relative contribution for each managerial function, as noted by the following symbols:

- ◎ defines factors with critical influence on the function
- ○ defines factors with some influence that could be remedied in later steps
- △ defines factors with relatively small influence

Such assessments were made for all functions. The relationships between departments and functions are summarized in Table 3-3.

The final business purpose at Toyota is to maximize long-range profit under various economic and environmental constraints. This long-range profit will be defined and expressed

Table 3-3. Summary of Various Functional Managements

Business Activity	Related Departments	Functions					
		Quality	Cost	Engineering	Production	Business	Personnel
Product Planning	• Product planning department • Engineering planning department	◎	◎	○	△	◎	○
Product Design	• Laboratory • Design department	◎	○	◎	○	○	○
Manufacturing Preparation	• Manufacturing engineering department • Manufacturing planning department	◎	◎	○	◎	△	○
Purchasing	• Purchasing department • Purchasing management department	◎	◎	△	△	△	○
Manufacturing	• Motomachi plant • Honsha plant	◎	○	△	◎	○	◎
Sales	• Sales department • Export department	◎	○	○	○	◎	○

Departmental Management

Functional Management

as a concrete figure through long-range business planning. Therefore, each function must be selected carefully and organized to be helpful in attaining the long-range profit.

If the number of functions was too high, then each function would begin to interfere with other functions, frustrating attempts to produce a new product in a timely and cost effective manner. Further, too many functions will foster strong independence of certain functions to the point that each departmental management might be enough to perform the function.

Conversely, if the number of functions was too small, too many departments would be related in a single function. Managing so many departments from a certain functional standpoint would be very complicated, if not impossible.

Toyota regards quality assurance and cost management as paramount functions, or *purpose functions*, and calls them the two pillars of functional management. Other functions are regarded as *means functions*. Thus, product planning and product design are integrated into an engineering function; manufacturing preparation and manufacturing into a production function; and sales and purchasing into a business function.

As a result, six functions remain in the Toyota functional management system, as illustrated in Table 3-3. In summary, each function in new product development, manufacturing technique, and marketing philosophy is not identical with other functions in its character or priority.

ORGANIZATION OF THE FUNCTIONAL MANAGEMENT SYSTEM

At Toyota, each director of the company is responsible for a certain department. Since each department involves more than one function, each director must participate in multiple functions, as we see in Table 3-3. No single director is responsible for a single function; he or she serves as a member of a team. Conversely, not all department directors participate in all functions. This would create difficulties managing each functional meeting because of too many members. For example, although there are thirteen departments involved in product planning and product design, only one or two directors will attend a QA functional meeting.

As previously stated, the functional meeting is the only formal organizational unit in functional management. Each functional meeting is a chartered decision-making unit charged to plan, check, and decide remedial actions required to achieve a functional goal. Each individual department serves as a line unit to perform the actions dictated by the functional meeting.

Figure 3-1 details the framework of the top management organization at Toyota. Each department is managed by a managing director or common director, whereas each functional meeting consists of all directors, including six executive directors. Since each executive director is responsible for integrating the actions of various departments, he or she will participate as chairperson in those functional meetings that have close relationships with that executive director's integrated departments. By necessity, even a vice president may participate in a functional meeting. A functional meeting typically numbers about ten members.

The QA and cost management functional meetings are conducted once a month. Generally, other functional meetings are held every other month. A functional meeting should not be convened without a significant agenda.

Functional meetings are positioned below the management meeting which consists of all managing directors and the standing auditor. The management meeting is an executive organization that gives final approval to the decisions of

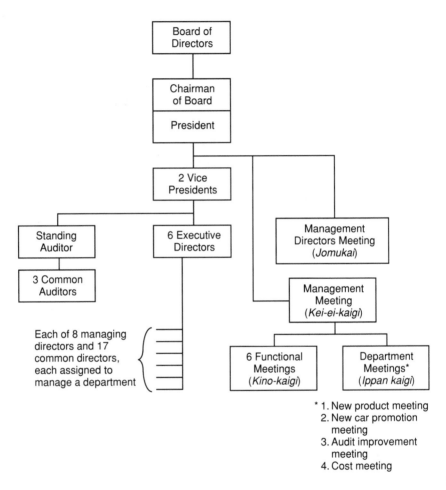

Figure 3-1. Framework of Toyota Management Organization (as of 1981)

the functional meeting. However, the essential decision-making authority remains with each functional meeting because implementation of the decision begins at the functional meeting. As long as there are no special objections in the management meeting, the decision made by the functional meeting will be treated as a company decision.

The *departmental meetings* shown in Figure 3-4 provide each department with a vehicle to discuss implementation of decisions made by the functional meeting. Note that the departmental meeting is not positioned as a substructure of the functional meeting. As with the functional meetings, plans for implementation generated within departmental meetings are subject to review and approval by the management meeting.

Occasionally, a problem arises such as a need to achieve a certain quality characteristic within a short-term period that cannot be resolved by only one functional meeting. By necessity, labor hours and costs must increase to improve the quality. At this time, a *joint functional meeting* combines quality and production functions. Further, in order to cope with a new legal restriction for safety and pollution, most of the functions, such as QA, cost, engineering, and production, must consider the restriction together. In this case, an *enlarged functional meeting* is formed to consider the problem. Note that these are not permanent organizational entities.

Another example involves a *cost management functional meeting*. Just after the oil shock in 1973, the profitability of the Toyota Corolla showed a marked decrease because of cost increases due to oil prices. At that time, the plant manager of Corolla made the following proposals to the cost functional meeting:

1. Promote a companywide cost reduction movement for Corolla.
2. Organize a Corolla Cost Reduction Committee chaired by the plant manager.
3. As substructures to this committee, organize the following sectional meetings:
   • production and assembly
   • design and engineering
   • purchasing

4. Establish a cost reduction of $40 per automobile.
5. Achieve the goal within six months.

Through a concerted effort by all departments based on the decisions of the cost management functional meeting, the actual result of the plan was 128 percent attainment of the goal at the end of six months (May 1975).

BUSINESS POLICY AND FUNCTIONAL MANAGEMENT

Since the introduction of the CWQC concept, a business policy has been developed and published. The policy applies to the operations level and includes each function previously discussed. The six elements of the business policy are shown in Figure 3-2 and defined in the following sections.

FUNDAMENTAL POLICY Fundamental policy is the business ethic principle, or fundamental directions, of the company. Once established, it will not change for many years.

An example is "Toyota wishes to develop in the world by collecting all powers inside and outside the company." The expression is abstract, but represents a business philosophy of top management. The fundamental policy is used to guide long-range planning.

LONG-TERM GOALS Long-term goals are goals to be attained within five years as an output of long-range planning. These goals are concrete figures expressed for production quality, sales quality, market share and return on investment (ROI), and so on.

LONG-TERM POLICY Long-term policy is the strategy used to achieve the long-term goals, and is expressed in more concrete detail than the fundamental policy. It covers several items common to the overall company.

For example: "In order to manage the overall company in a scientific manner, policies, goals, and plans must be prepared for each department and a control point must be defined clearly and directed."

ANNUAL SLOGANS   Annual slogans are a means for Toyota to emphasize annual policies. The purpose of these slogans is to encourage a sound mental attitude in all employees and there are two types.

The first type remains the same every year, such as "Assure the quality in every Toyota." The second type emphasizes the policy for the year. For example, the 1974 slogan after the oil shock was "Build Toyotas for the changing age." Also: "It is time to use scarce resources effectively."

ANNUAL GOALS OF EACH FUNCTION   Accepting the long-term goals just described, the annual goals of each function to be achieved within the current year must be expressed in specific figures. These goal figures are established for each function. Each functional meeting, in turn, decides how to achieve these goals. The items included as annual goals for each function follow:

- *Overall Company:* ROI, production quantity, and market share
- *Production:* rate of reduced manpower to previous year's manpower level
- *Quality:* rate of reduction of problems in the marketplace
- *Cost:* total amount of costs to be reduced, plant and equipment investment amount, and margin rates of the preferentially developed automobiles
- *Safety, sanitation, and environment:* number of closures for holidays, and so on, at business and plants

ANNUAL WORKING PLANS OF EACH FUNCTION
Once annual goals are established for each function, annual
working plans of each function must be determined by the
appropriate functional meeting. Implementation of these
working plans then becomes the responsibility of the department meeting.

Classification of the functions shown in Figure 3-2 differs
somewhat from that presented in Table 3-3 because the business policy must describe all the important topics to be
achieved in the current year. The business function in Table
3-3 is incorporated into the overall company function shown
in Figure 3-2, which also includes information and public
relations. Further, although the safety, sanitation, and environment functions are not shown in Table 3-3, nor is there a
functional meeting, safety and environment are included

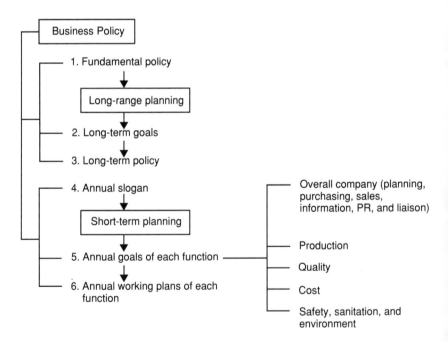

Figure 3-2. Six Elements of Business Policy at Toyota

with the production functional meeting, while sanitation is included with both the production and personnel functions.

EXTENSION OF BUSINESS POLICY

Formal announcement of the business policy at Toyota is made by the president in his New Year's greetings to the employees. Extension plans of each function are issued to each department by the office of the functional meeting. Department policies and plans then are formulated by the department meeting.

After implementation of these plans, the results of actual performance are evaluated during the middle and at the end of the current year. Feedback from these evaluations are used to form the policies for the next year. Such checks and evaluations are made at three levels within the organization: operations checks of selected topics by top management, functional checks by each functional meeting chairperson, and department checks by each department manager or director. Figure 3-3 shows the organization planning and control system employed at Toyota.

CRITICAL CONSIDERATIONS FOR FUNCTIONAL MANAGEMENT

Four critical considerations demand special attention in order to achieve a successful functional management program:

1. Select important functions carefully to properly balance department participation. Too many departments in the same functional meeting lead to confusion and difficulties managing the meeting. Too few member departments create a need for many individual functions that will begin to overlap responsibilities, again creating confusion and management problems.
2. Do not regard functional management as an informal system. The position and guidelines of functional

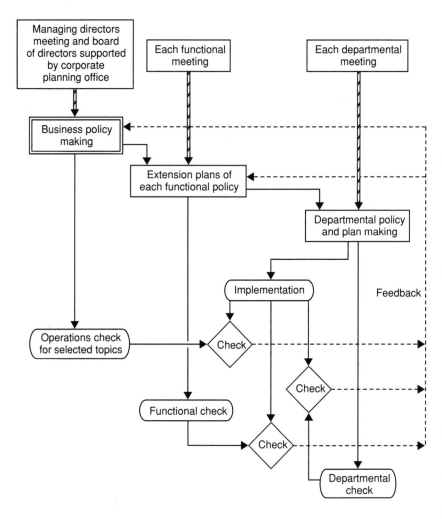

Figure 3-3. Toyota Planning and Control System

meetings in the top management scheme must be defined clearly. The functional meeting must receive the necessary authority to implement its decisions as company policy.

3. Each line department must have a strong structure in place to execute the plans put forth by the various meetings.
4. The director in charge of each function is also the head of a department. This individual, however, must formulate and direct the function for the overall company, not for a particular department.

ADVANTAGES OF FUNCTIONAL MANAGEMENT

Functional management as implemented at Toyota offers certain advantages not found in other management systems. For example:

- Both policies and implementation are decisive and rapidly instituted. This results because the functional meeting is a substantive decision-making entity with responsibilities and authority directed from top management. In addition, communication to executing line departments is rapid since members of the functional meeting are also directors responsible for related departments.
- *Nemawashi* is unnecessary at Toyota. The original meaning of this term comes from the preparations for transplanting a large tree. One must dig around the roots, cutting larger ones so that smaller roots run to secure its new position. In business, *nemawashi* refers to the persuasion of related individuals, such as management executives, prior to a formal decision-making meeting. At Toyota, the functional meeting itself becomes the *nemawashi* negotiation.
- Functional meetings serve to enhance communications and human relations among the various depart-

ments because all sides are brought together to achieve a common goal.

- Communications from subordinate employees to the functional meetings are achieved easily because there is no need for prior persuasion. Employees bring their suggestions and ideas to their department managers for discussion at the functional meetings.

CHAPTER 4

Flat Organizational
and Personnel Management

IN RECENT YEARS, diversifying customer needs, technological progress, internationalization, and other trends have created a fast-changing business environment to which companies must learn to respond flexibly and swiftly.

Company organizations can respond effectively to the needs of this changing environment in two ways:

The first is by accelerating the decision-making process; that is, the events that occur between recognizing the need for a decision and establishing the final decision. We call the time period for these events the "decision-making lead time." If a company can shorten its decision-making lead time, it is then better able to (1) take advantage of new business opportunities, (2) carry out more timely new product development, and (3) respond more promptly and effectively to any customer complaints that arise. We can think of this type of improvement as implementing the just-in-time approach within the decision-making process.

Second, companies should cultivate among employees an ambition to accept challenges. In many cases, popular products result from a company organization that encourages younger, freer-thinking employees to be assertive in proposing their own ideas. It is especially important for companies in mature or declining industries to give free rein to employee ingenuity in developing ideas for new fields of business.

This chapter studies the various methods that Toyota uses to speed up its decision-making process and cultivate the challenging employee talents and abilities, enabling the company to respond more flexibly and swiftly to our fast-changing business environment. The following observations should help make us more conscious of just how important and universal this new theme in organizational management is for companies today.

In Figure 4-1, I have outlined the reforms that Toyota has made recently in its corporate organization and personnel system. We will examine these reforms one by one in order.

ACCELERATING THE DECISION-MAKING PROCESS THROUGH REORGANIZATION

On August 1, 1989, Toyota implemented a new organization structure. The principle objective of this reorganization was to speed up the decision-making process.[1] This new organization did away with the traditional pyramid structure of middle-management ranks and replaced it with a flatter structure that has fewer layers and is centered on offices within each department that are supervised by only two layers: office chiefs and the department chief. (See Figure 4-2.)

Prior to this reorganization, Toyota's middle management included numerous layers that included the department chief, deputy department chief, supervisors, section chiefs, assistant section chiefs, and chief clerks. There are now only three layers — department chief, office chiefs, and group leaders.

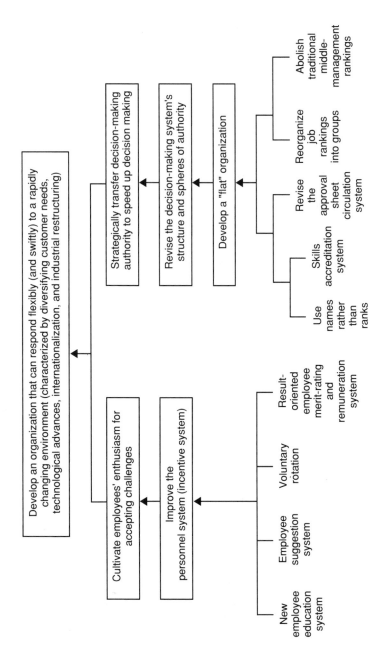

Figure 4-1. Reforms to Accelerate Decision-making

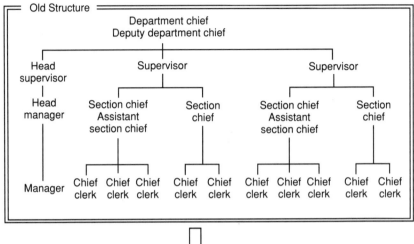

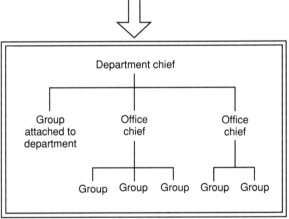

Figure 4-2. Reorganization of Middle Management at Toyota

In addition to reducing the number of layers in the middle-management structure, the new "office-based" structure consolidates what used to be two or three departments into each office. The groups in these offices are able to reorganize themselves with flexibility whenever such regrouping is deemed necessary by the department chief. Membership in these groups is open to a wide range of people, from department chiefs to ordinary employees.

The only type of group whose position has yet to be defined clearly is the "group attached to department" type shown in Figure 4-2.

Toyota implemented this organizational reform in all of its clerical and engineering departments except for those in overseas offices and in plant-based production departments. As a result, some 20,000 of Toyota's roughly 67,000 employees were directly affected by this reorganization.

From my own perspective, I find the following advantages in switching from a multi-layered pyramid structure to this simpler and flatter structure.

1. It speeds up the decision-making process by streamlining the approval sheet circulation system (the *ringi* system) to reduce both the number of managers at each rank and the number of managerial ranks that receive the approval sheet.

2. Decision-making authority is no longer spread so far vertically and horizontally in the management structure but is restricted instead to group leaders and their superiors. Clearly defined guidelines have been created to regulate the transfer of authority.

3. The number of middle-management positions has been reduced by about half, which makes it easier for lower-level employees to get their ideas across to top managers. In other words, it creates in a more streamlined and direct course for the bottom-up flow of information in the company. As a result, younger employees are encouraged to propose ideas to their higher-ups.

4. Requests and complaints from customers also travel more easily through the organizational ranks to top management. This helps Toyota live up to its "customers first" philosophy.

5. Upper-level managers used to spend a lot of time supervising the various ranks of middle managers and

had little opportunity to develop specific skills. The new group-based structure enables the managers and employees of individual groups to develop higher levels of knowledge and technical skill thus raising the quality of their own work.

While the number of people in one office may range from thirty to one hundred, the average office is made up of about fifty people. Their work includes routine work, strategic work, and work based on various types of project themes, both large and small.

The new rank of office chief, while primarily made up of former supervisors, include former department chiefs and section chiefs. The group leaders, while mostly former section chiefs, also include some assistant department chiefs and chief clerks. The people selected for specific project themes represent a wide range of backgrounds and qualifications.

To maintain this new organization's flexibility and enthusiasm, the personnel department promotes close communication among department chiefs, office chiefs, and other managers, and downplays rank status as a barrier to such communication.

All together, there were some 6,200 department chiefs, deputy department chiefs, section chiefs, and chief clerks whose ranks were changed by this reorganization.

The number of departments at Toyota increased slightly, from 173 before the reorganization to 177 afterward. While the number of departments did not change much, the number of sections was reduced by two-thirds and lower management positions within the sections were cut by about half. The group leaders were the most active rank in the decision-making process. The number of section chiefs and chief clerks, who traditionally had more passive roles, fell from about 2,000 persons to a little over 1,000.

In addition, Toyota made other department-level organizational changes that broadened employee training to include hiring, job assignment, benefits, and training to develop an organization better able to respond to international operations in various countries.[2] Toyota reorganized both the personnel and education departments, renaming the latter the human resources development department. It then established a third department called the international personnel department.

Another new department established at this time was the Motor Sports Department, whose main purpose is to boost Toyota's activities in motor sports and to help promote the company's technological development.

CHANGES IN THE APPROVAL SHEET SYSTEM

In August 1988, exactly one year before the organizational changes described above were made, Toyota launched what it called a three stamp campaign. Until then, approval sheets concerning management decisions had required seven or eight different people to sign off by affixing their name stamps *(hanko)*. Developers of the campaign found that the number of people who need to receive such approval sheets could be reduced responsibly to just three, hence the name for their improvement scheme. Gradually, this campaign became a means to prepare for the major organizational changes of the following year. The three stamp campaign had the following three goals:

1. Speed up the decision-making process.
2. Train lower-ranked managers by delegating more responsibility to their areas.
3. Improve morale.

The following describes some of the advantages and disadvantages of the conventional approval sheet system.[3]

Because the conventional approval sheet system tended to concentrate authority in the upper management ranks, Toyota found it difficult to delegate more authority to middle and lower managers.

As more items require approval sheets, less authority (and, therefore, less responsibility) is given to section chiefs and other lower-ranked managers. In many cases, if the decision has poor results, responsibility for the mistake does not stop with the high-ranked person on the approval sheet but extends to the person or persons who proposed the decision in the first place. When the managers who need to sign off are many and spread among several departments or management levels, it tends to take longer to reach a consensus in approving the decision.

Under the *flat organization* scheme, Toyota has aimed to reduce the number of items that require approval sheets while also reducing the variety (ranks) and number of managers who must receive the sheets.

The three stamp campaign has helped clarify the decision-making criteria for each level of management at Toyota. By decision-making criteria, we mean such matters as who has the right to propose decisions, who such decision items must be submitted to for approval, and who has the final decision-making authority.

However, even streamlining the approval sheet system leaves a number of problems. For instance, the following three problems relate to the budgeting system.[4]

INADEQUATE DELEGATION OF AUTHORITY

For example, a sales section chief is given a certain amount of freedom, within the budgeted allowance, to charge the company for client entertainment expenses. Although the section chief generally is responsible for how the budgeted expense allowance is spent, he or she needs the division chief's approval for any expense items that exceed the per-item cost ceiling — and therefore does not have full authority over the expense account.

ITEMS OUTSIDE OF BUDGET

This type of problem exists in any kind of budgeting system, whether or not it follows the conventional approval system format. *Items outside of budget* refers to expense items that were not anticipated when the budget was planned. Such items must be approved separately via some kind of special-case approval system. Alternatively, they can be handled by a committee whose responsibilities specifically include the formal processing of items outside of budget.

ITEMS THAT REQUIRE SPECIAL TREATMENT

As an example, plant investment budgets generally allocate a certain amount of funds for the year. However, often it is uncertain what kinds of projects will be claiming some of these funds in the year's third and/or fourth quarter. When deciding upon such projects, the managers responsible for planning them must submit approval sheets and receive prior approval from higher-ups. Other types of major expense items that may require similar special treatment include major repair schemes and sales publicity campaigns. Generally, it may be a good idea to have an approval sheet system for certain activities (such as publicity campaigns), when those activities are initially given a very loose budget framework to work within. This would help activity planners be more flexible in responding to current conditions.

SKILLS ACCREDITATION SYSTEM AND USE OF NAMES INSTEAD OF RANKS

Although the implementation of the new flat organization did away with certain management ranks such as section chief and chief clerk, those job titles are still being used in the skills accreditation system.

At Toyota, all promotions, salaries, and job titles for use outside the company are based on the individual's skills accreditation level and not on his or her current job assignment.

Toyota had introduced its skills accreditation system in November 1987. This system had established skill levels called councillor, vice councillor, and competent authority. However, when the flat organization was established, the skill level titles were changed to department chief class, supervisor class, section chief class, chief clerk class, and so on.

On the business cards for presentation to customers and other outside contacts, the managers who have reached the section chief class in the skills accreditation system are identified as "chief of XXX section, XXX department." Likewise, those who have reached the chief clerk level in skills accreditation are described as "chief clerk of XXX section, XXX department." In other words, even though there are no longer any of the old multilayered sections in the organization, the company has retained the old section-based titles for formal purposes — such as on business cards.

Why bother with such formalities? Mainly, it is for the sake of convenience. Japanese society is still a rank-oriented society, and if Toyota's managers were to dispense with the traditional management rankings, they would find it more difficult to assure their customers and other contacts outside the company of their position and authority within Toyota.

Meanwhile, internally Toyota is trying to become less rank-oriented. This is not only by introducing the new flat organization, but also by encouraging employees to address their higher-ups by their names (for example, Mr. Yamada or Ms. Aoki) instead of by their rank, which has been the custom. This was done to help the new flat organization achieve one of its goals — to make it easier for lower-level managers to get their ideas across to higher-ups, especially in view of the fact that it is often the younger employees who have the original ideas for new hit products.

As such, this new way of addressing managers recognizes that a flat organization alone will not improve the decision-making process much if there still exists an atmosphere that stifles the free expression of ideas. In addition, the act of changing customs by calling managers by their names helps employees to change their way of thinking about the organization. It helps them feel personally involved in the reform process.

It has been suggested, however, that the retention of traditional ranks for use outside the company dampens this new, reform-minded way of thinking.[5] Such critics point out that ordinary employees find it difficult to ignore a person's ranking when the employee knows that person still carries a traditional ranking, at least on his or her business card.

In any case, one would have to admit that it is not very easy to buck tradition and establish a new mode for human relationships.

REFORMING THE PERSONNEL SYSTEM TO CULTIVATE THE CHALLENGING EMPLOYEE

Despite the previously described factors that were designed to help employees change their way of thinking, simply changing the structure of an organization is rarely enough to revitalize the organization. Instead, a new system must be established that inspires people within the organization to get personally involved in its revitalization.

As mentioned earlier, today's business environment is one in which companies must come up with fresh ideas that meet with diversifying customer needs. At the same time, companies must maintain a forward-thinking R&D program to keep pace with rapidly advancing high technologies and developing employee skills, both to meet the challenges of corporate internationalization and overseas operations and to develop and promote ideas for new business ventures.

The term *incentive systems* is used to describe systems that are designed to promote employee enthusiasm and confidence in accepting these kinds of challenges. Toyota has introduced the following four incentive systems:[6]

1. a personnel merit-rating and compensation system to emphasize results
2. voluntary rotation
3. an in-house suggestion system for recruiting
4. a new employee education system

The previous personnel merit-rating system, which had been based on seniority and accumulated merit, was changed to emphasize the evaluation of job performance in recent months and years. In addition, the previous overall evaluation system was made more specific by dividing evaluation into (1) merit during the past year (reflected in the size of the two semiannual bonuses), which looks at what kinds of projects have been undertaken and the results achieved, and (2) skill merit based on what specialist skills the employee has worked toward mastering (reflected in promotions to higher ranks).

Currently, the higher-ranked employees generally evaluate their subordinates in terms of factors such as job performance, character, and teamwork skills. In April 1990, a new job performance evaluation method was added to this same general evaluation method. It entails that once yearly each employee meets with his or her superior to discuss and establish job performance targets. At the end of the business year, they meet again to evaluate job performance in reaching the targets set for that year.

In determining the size of employee salaries, Toyota applies these job performance evaluation results as 10 percent of the total evaluation score, while a higher percentage is applied to determining bonuses. This means that job performance now plays a direct role in assessing employee remuneration in terms of semiannual bonuses.[7] Toyota has applied this new assessment system to all of its clerical and research departments. The new system's mechanism of assessing employee remuneration based partly on achieving job performance targets has made everyone aware of a new emphasis on skills and results.

As for voluntary rotation, Toyota employees who have been working in the same department or section for at least five years are able to apply for transfer (rotation) to their preferred department. Generally, the company is able to accommodate the employee's rotation request within two years. As such, this system supports employees' desires to pursue the job challenges that interest them most.

With the in-house suggestion system, Toyota actively seeks out employee ideas as the company considers expanding into promising new fields of business, such as motor sports and leisure-related businesses. Also employees who want to promote new businesses are invited to remain with the company.

In February 1989, Toyota established a *business development office* to promote new business expansion outside its main business. In May 1989, all managers ranked at the section chief level or higher were asked to submit suggestions for new business ideas. This campaign generated some 700 suggestions.

In broad terms, Toyota's new employee education system relates to the company's entire organizational reform program.

Specifically, however, it relates to efforts to promote educational exchanges with companies in other industries to help broaden and deepen specialist skills among managers.

IMPROVING THE OFFICE ENVIRONMENT — LAYOUT IMPROVEMENT

In 1990, Toyota adopted a three-year plan to invest roughly ¥ 5 billion per year to improve the work environment in its offices.[8] Intended to help reinvigorate the organization, this campaign was launched as part of a program to reevaluate various office facilities, raise the operational efficiency in offices, and boost employee morale.

Toyota already had begun the same program on an experimental basis in August 1988 at its head office (Toyoda City, Aichi Prefecture) and at other offices, including its Tokyo branch office (Bunkyo-ku, Tokyo) and its North America office. This experimental program proved successful, which led Toyota to implement it companywide.

Specifically, in August 1988 Toyota changed the layout of its personnel department offices located on the fifth floor of the No. 1 head office building. In the new layout, the desk of the chief personnel officer (Director Isomura) was placed in the center of the large (about 840 square meters) main floor. The desks of the various department and office chiefs were placed around it, followed by rows of the other employee desks.

Compared to the previous layout, which had executives' desks lined up along the sides of the room with lower-ranked employees' desks sandwiched in the middle, the lower-ranked employees preferred the improved layout. They felt it was easier for them to communicate. In addition, some of the conventional rectangular desks were replaced with more stylish round or oval desks, and the office automation equipment was upgraded.

EMPLOYEES' EVALUATION OF TOYOTA'S
PERSONNEL ORGANIZATION REFORMS

The following information was taken from the responses to a questionnaire that Toyota circulated among some of its employees to determine how well its major organizational and personnel system reforms were accepted.[9]

The questionnaire asked participants to evaluate the organizational reforms. It was circulated among 2,500 randomly selected employees ranked from ordinary employee to department chief. Questionnaire results were announced on November 11, 1989.

Roughly 70 percent of the department chiefs (about 500 people) felt that the new flat organization gave more decision-making authority to their subordinates. Meanwhile, 60 percent of all respondents felt their way of working had changed as a result of the reforms. Likewise, 60 percent of all respondents reported that they had followed the suggestion of the campaign to downplay rank and had begun calling managers by their names instead of their rank. In addition, about 80 percent of all respondents said they were implementing the new policy of requiring only three name stamps on approval sheets as recommended by the three stamp campaign.

These results assured Toyota's top managers that their organizational reforms were a success.

CONCLUSION

The major organizational and personnel system reforms undertaken by Toyota have removed, with surgical precision, much of the fat and lethargy that is symptomatic of the large corporation syndrome. As a result, the traditional pyramid-shaped organizational structure has been flattened out considerably, with more decision-making authority accorded to middle- and lower-management people, while making it easier for everyone, including the youngest employees, to communicate their ideas assertively to superiors. All of these changes have helped make Toyota's organization more efficient, flexible, and energetic in its responses to today's rapidly changing environment.

CHAPTER 5

Sales Management System

The sales volume and market share of any particular product is determined by the product's sales strength and the company's sales strength.

In considering the product's sales strength, the most important factor is how well the product's developers have anticipated user trends such as changing social conditions and lifestyles. Sometimes, a single product has enough sales strength to pull its company from behind into the lead against the competition. This happened in Japan when Asahi Breweries marketed its "Super Dry" beer and when Nissan introduced its "Cima" line of luxury cars. We will study Toyota's new product development system in Chapter 6.

As for the company's sales strength, the prime determinant of sales volume is the number of sales outlets and the number of salespeople. This can be termed the company's quantitative sales strength. However, it is also important to consider how powerful each sales outlet's sales activities are; in other words, how stimulated and energized the staff at each sales office is by the challenge of taking on the competition. This we call the company's qualitative sales strength.

In this chapter we will examine the key factors behind Toyota's quantitative and qualitative sales strengths, focusing on the characteristics of Toyota's sales network and sales channels.

CHARACTERISTICS OF TOYOTA'S SALES NETWORK

QUANTITATIVE STRENGTH

The secret of Toyota's powerful sales network lies in its massive size and its high quality, both of which are the legacy of a Mr. Shōtarō Kamiya.

Toyota Motor was born from a loom manufacturing company known as Toyoda Automatic Loom Works. This company began trial production of passenger cars in 1934.* In October 1935, company president Kiichirō Toyoda lured Shōtarō Kamiya away from Nippon GM and gave him the job of marketing Toyota's new cars. Later, when Toyota split into the manufacturing company Toyota Motor Company and the sales company Toyota Motor Sales, Kamiya was installed as the latter company's president, and was so successful that he earned the nickname "the god of sales." When Kamiya quit Nippon GM to join Toyota, he brought along two of his subordinates: Shikanosuke Hanazaki and Taneyuki Kato. Kamiya also managed to talk several of Nippon GM's Chevrolet and Buick sales outlets into switching over to the Toyota Group.

Meanwhile, Nissan followed Toyota's lead two years later by recruiting Sadajiro Ashida from Nippon GM to help establish Nissan Auto Sales. Since Toyota had already picked through the GM dealers for converts, Nissan approached Ford dealers about joining the Nissan group, but had little

---

* In Japanese, the family name "Toyoda" means "abundant rice field." In 1936 a contest was held to choose a more marketable name for the new automobiles — and "Toyota" was chosen.

success. From that time on, Nissan clearly lagged behind Toyota in terms of sales strength.

Kamiya's basic policy concerning sales outlets was to follow Ford and GM's lead in establishing one dealer franchise per prefecture. In addition, Kamiya worked to establish a network of independent specialist sales outlets to be set up using local capital and local citizenry. These policies remain fundamental to Toyota's sales network even today.

President Kamiya once remarked that the reason Toyota was able to lure away so many of Nippon GM's sales outlets was because these sales outlets resented Nippon GM because of its failure to use local capital and its single-minded pursuit of big profits. He felt that the proper relationship between car manufacturers and dealers should be one of mutual prosperity. This sales philosophy still lives at Toyota. It is safe to say that a company that follows an excellent business philosophy is best assured of success and prosperity.

These developments eventually led to the founding of Toyota Motor Company in August 1937.

During World War II, automobiles came under a rationing system established by the wartime government. In 1942, the Nippon Automobile Distribution Company *(Nippon Jidosha Haikyu Kabushiki Kaisha)* was established. Known as *Nichihai* for short, this company established regional affiliates called regional automobile distribution companies *(chiho jidosha haikyu kabushiki kaisha)*, or *Jihai* for short, that grouped together car dealers belonging to the various manufacturers' groups. The military had first pick of all automobiles that left the nation's factories. Nichihai then bought up whatever inventory was left over and distributed the vehicles to the various Jihai companies. They in turn sold them to private-sector buyers. Kamiya was assigned to Nichihai as a managing director in charge of the vehicle division.

The postwar Ministry of Transport dissolved the Nichihai/Jihai network in June 1946, and authorized the reestablishment of the manufacturer sales networks that had existed prior to the war. At that time, the reborn Toyota Group welcomed back the able salespeople who had run their sales outlets earlier. In addition, Toyota managed to win over several former Nissan salespeople.

It is no exaggeration to say that the current domestic share gap between Toyota and Nissan began during that decisive period in postwar Japan. During the war, Kamiya made it clear to the other Nichihai leaders that sales people depended upon demand and manufacturers depended upon sales people. This philosophy was enshrined in Kamiya's famous dictum: *The customer comes first, the dealer second, and the manufacturer third.* This was the type of thinking that attracted so many dealers to Toyota when the new dealership groups were reestablished. In a sense, Kamiya already had dealt a decisive blow to his competitors even before the battle began.

In this way, Toyota outperformed the competition and, as of 1988, accumulated 4,333 sales outlets, staffed by some

Table 5-1. Sales Forces of Major Japanese Automakers

	Sales Companies	Sales Outlets	No. of Salespeople
Toyota	314	4,333	40,600
Nissan	243	3,020	28,000
Mazda	111	1,589	12,000
Mitsubishi	333	1,296	9,000
Honda	1,610*	2,260	7,600

* This figure includes 1,400 "Primo" companies. Other industry estimates for number of salespeople: 5,000 for Daihatsu, 3,500 for Fuji Heavy Industries (Subaru), and 3,300 for Suzuki Motors.

40,600 well-trained salespeople. Compare this to 28,000 sales-people for Nissan and 12,000 for Mazda.

As shown in Table 5-1, the expansion of Toyota's sales network did not happen in sudden leaps and bounds. Rather, much of it resulted directly from the diligent and well-timed efforts of Kamiya over a period of many years. This kind of expansion is not subject to the sudden reversals of fortune that can be seen in product sales strength. The key to Toyota's steady sales network expansion over the past few decades has been an emphasis not only on increasing the number of sales outlets and sales staff but also on enriching and strengthening these outlets by providing excellent guidance and training.

EXCLUSIVE DEALERSHIP AND TERRITORY SYSTEM

All of Japan's automakers have established a franchise system based on exclusive dealerships and territories. The first to build such a system was Toyota, under the leadership of Shōtarō Kamiya.

The exclusive dealerships have the following features:

- The manufacturer markets its products exclusively through sales companies (dealerships) that handle only that manufacturer's products.
- The manufacturer forbids the dealerships from handling any other manufacturer's products.
- The manufacturer ensures that the dealership is the sole agency for the manufacturer's products within a certain area.

The territory system has the following features:

- The manufacturer defines the borders of each dealership's sales territory.

- Dealership sales territories can be defined either as closed territories, which allow the presence of only one dealer, or as open territories, which allow the presence of several dealers. Japanese automobile companies have all opted for open territories.

Having sales companies that belong to the manufacturer's group of affiliated companies *(keiretsu)* and having a territory system are both methods by which Japanese auto companies organize the distribution of their products.

In Toyota's case, the sales affiliates are divided into five groups, each based on a major model line of Toyota cars. (Nissan also has a five-pronged sales affiliate organization.) This kind of arrangement sometimes is called a "multidealer sales organization."

The following are Toyota's five groups of dealers and the product models handled by each group. (Domestic market product names are used here.)

1. Toyota dealerships: Crown, Century, Carina, Soarer
2. Toyopet dealerships: Mark II, Corona, Corsa, Soarer
3. Corolla dealerships: Celica, Camry, Corolla, Corolla II
4. Auto dealerships: Chaser, Sprinter, Starlet
5. Vista dealerships: Cresta, Vista, Tercel

This system maintains almost completely model-specific dealership groups, thereby reducing competition among the groups.

The chief model handled by Toyota dealerships is the top-of-the-line Crown luxury sedan, which is sold primarily to companies.

At Toyopet dealerships, the biggest sellers are the Mark II and Corona models. The Mark II is Toyota's top-of-the-line family car, aimed primarily at individual consumers in the 35- to 45-year age group. The Corona is Toyota's top-of-the-line compact car, aimed at both families and young people.

Corolla dealerships are named after their chief seller, the Corolla. This is also Toyota's biggest seller overall, aimed at families and young people.

Auto dealerships mainly handle the Sprinter, Toyota's highest grade car for the general public.

Vista dealers also are named after their main model, which is a new type of mass-market car seen as the next generation to the Corolla.

Thus, each dealership has its main model, a limited selection of other models, and operates within a well-defined territory. Generally, there is only one dealership for each of the above five groups in each prefecture, although there are two or more in the major metropolitan prefectures. This means that five Toyota dealerships, one from each group, operate in the same territory within what we referred to earlier as an open territory system.

This type of sales organization is particularly beneficial for dealerships that handle the most popular models. On the other hand, it works against the interest of the dealerships that handle the least popular models. It also means that model changes tend to have a big impact on the dealerships. These facts have led Toyota to introduce its *mutual-aid system* whereby dealerships in different groups agree to share certain models. For example, a Toyota dealer that handles mainly Crown passenger models might agree to let the local Toyopet dealer handle all of its Crown commercial models. To reciprocate, the Toyopet allows the Toyota dealer to handle its Corona commercial models. This kind of arrangement offers several advantages:

1. It lessens the impact of a model change (including a minor change) on a specific dealership group by spreading it out among two or more groups. Without the mutual-aid system, dealerships facing a model change would find themselves hard put to sell current

Table 5-2. Toyota's Sales and Service Network

Models handled	Toyota dealers (T)	Tokyo Toyota	Aichi Toyota	Osaka Toyota	Okinawa Toyota	Toyopet dealers (P)	Tokyo Toyopet	Osaka Toyopet	Toyota Corolla dealers (C)	Nagoya Toyota Diesel	Toyota Auto dealers (A)	Tokyo District Toyota Auto	Osaka District Toyota Auto	Okinawa Toyota Auto	Toyota Vista dealers (V)	Toyota Forklift dealers	Toyota Lease companies
		Also includes:					*Also includes:*			*Also includes:*		*Also includes:*					*Handles all Toyota models*
Passenger cars																	
Century	●	•	•	•	•		•	•									
Crown	●	•	•	◀	•		•	•									
Soarer	●	•	•	•	•	●	•	•									
Supra		•		•													
Mark II						●	■										
Chaser					•												
Cresta					•						●	•	•	•	●		
Camry										•		◀		•	●		
Vista																	
Corona	●	•			•	●		•	●	•							
Carina		■	•	•			■										
Celica							•		●	•							
Corolla									●	•	●	•	•	•			
Sprinter							•							•			
Corsa				•		●			●	•							
Corolla II																	
Tercel														•	●		
Starlet											●	•	•	•			

Handles all Toyota models

Trucks

- Toyota MR2
- Sprinter Carib
- Dyna
- Toyoace
- Hiace
- Master Ace
- Town Ace
- Liteace
- Hilux
- Publica Pick-up
- Land Cruiser
- Blizzard
- Coaster
- Industrial vehicles

1. Solid squares indicate dealers that handle only passenger cars and solid triangles dealers that handle only vans.
2. Toyota industrial vehicle dealers include 32 Toyota Forklift dealers. The Toyota dealer handles districts that do not have their own Toyota Forklift dealer (except for the Tokushima District, which is handled by a Toyopet dealer).

[Translator's Note: The above car model names are those used in Japan. Some of these models may use different names in overseas markets.]

models just prior to the introduction of the new model. They would feel pressured to resort to absorption sales and their business results would have bigger fluctuations. By contrast, the mutual-aid system enables the impact of model changes to be spread out. That, plus the fact that each dealership group handles several models, helps spread the sales risks associated with specific models.

2. The mutual-aid system also makes for a more extensive network for parts supply and after-sales service. Again using the previous example of mutual aid in Crown and Corona sales, both dealerships are required to maintain parts supply and after-sales service for both car models. This results in a broader-ranging and stronger after-sales service organization.

Table 5-2 shows the specific relationships between dealership groups and car models handled.

COMPETITION AMONG DEALERSHIP GROUPS

Formally, there is no competition between Toyota dealerships in the same territory, since each belongs to a different group and sells different models aimed at different consumer strata. However, the fact is that the expansion of Toyota's selection of models has caused overlapping among targeted consumer strata. This in turn has led to increasingly severe competition among Toyota dealerships belonging to different groups in the same territory. In other words, the dealership groups are not as distinctive from each other as they used to be.

Let us take as an example the Kanagawa Toyota dealership, which was established in October 1946. This was Toyota's first dealership in Kanagawa Prefecture following the war. Noting the principle that one cup can only hold one cup's worth of

water, Toyota's Kamiya decided to set up a second sales channel for Toyota cars in the region by establishing the first
Toyopet dealership in the region's main city of Yokohama in
January 1956. Later, the Kanagawa Toyota and Yokohama
Toyopet dealerships jointly invested their own capital to establish a Corolla dealership for the region in 1961, then an Auto
dealership in 1968, and finally a Vista dealership in 1979. Over
the years, the competition among these Toyota dealerships in
the same territory has steadily increased.

Obviously, competition among dealerships in the same territories is a positive factor for Toyota's overall sales and is a key
factor behind the strength of the Toyota sales organization.

ADVANTAGES OF USING LOCAL CAPITAL

Of the 314 sales companies (and 4,333 sales outlets) in the
Toyota group, Toyota directly owns (by direct equity investment) only thirteen companies. The other 301 sales companies
(about 96 percent of the total) were established using local
capital. The thirteen wholly owned sales companies consist of
six Tokyo-based companies (including Tokyo Toyota, Tokyo
Toyopet, and Tokyo Corolla), one company based in Osaka
(Osaka Toyopet), five in Sapporo, and one in Fukuoka.

By contrast, nationally, Japan's automakers held full ownership of 20 percent of their sales companies on average,
majority ownership (ranging from 50 to 99 percent of sales
company equity) in another 11 percent, and minority ownership (less than 50 percent of sales company equity) in another
19 percent. The industry average thus shows that exclusively
local capitalization is the case at half of Japan's auto sales
companies. By and large, these locally capitalized sales companies are invested in by prominent local companies.

When we subtract Toyota, who owns only one-tenth of its
sales companies, from the industry average, we see that the

remaining Japanese automakers own on average over 60 percent of their sales companies. The only other automaker whose ownership level is anywhere near as low as Toyota's is the relatively small-scaled competitor, Honda.

Toyota's emphasis on having local business interests capitalize its regional sales companies was part of the sales expansion policy developed early on by Kamiya. This policy reaped the following advantages.

The local managers running these regional sales companies are more serious about succeeding when they know that local business interests have their money invested in these sales companies.

Local ownership also makes it easier for profits to be reinvested in the sales companies that earn them. After all, most managers at sales companies that are fully owned by the parent automaker are employees on loan from the parent company. They tend to think profits should be channeled back to the parent company. Also, they tend to be less concerned with the regional sales company's long-term interests.

The sales power of locally owned regional sales companies is boosted by double support — support from the parent company and support from local investors and the local people who make up almost all of the sales company management.

In addition, the fact that these regional sales companies are owned and operated almost entirely by local people makes it easier to increase sales through social and family ties in the community.

ADVANTAGES OF WHOLLY OWNED DEALERSHIPS

As mentioned earlier, Toyota has thirteen wholly owned dealerships. Most of these are in the two largest metropolitan prefectures of Tokyo and Osaka, where competition among dealerships is the greatest.